Legacy of Excellence

Mario Lemieux's Impact on the Penguins and the City of Pittsburgh

By

Jason Zemcik

Copyright © 2017 by Jason Zemcik

All rights reserved. No part of this book may be reproduced, distributed, or transmitted in any form or by any means, including photocopying, recording, screenshotting via electronic reading devices, or any other electronic or mechanical method without prior written permission from Jason Zemcik. The only allowable exception to this is for brief quotations used in critical reviews or certain other noncommercial uses permitted under copyright law.

Cover design by Jason Zemcik.

About the Author

Jason Zemcik is a lifelong Penguins, Steelers, and Pirates fan who was born and raised in Somerset, Pennsylvania. He has written and published multiple books about his favorite Pittsburgh teams as well as one about the Holly Springs (North Carolina) Salamanders Coastal Plain League baseball team, a collegiate summer league squad, and one about his hobby of collecting hockey jerseys.

His writing has also been featured on the Pittsburgh Post-Gazette website, CityofChampionsSports.com, and MLBCenter.com.

He currently lives outside of Raleigh, North Carolina with his wife and daughter.

You can connect with him on Facebook (@jasonzemcikauthor) and Twitter (@JasonZemcik) to stay up to date on all of his latest writing.

Also by Jason Zemcik

Pittsburgh Sports

Black and Gold Dynasty Series: The Championship History of the Pittsburgh Steelers

PENSational: How the 2015-16 Pittsburgh Penguins Captivated an Entire City on Their Way to Winning the Stanley Cup

Buc to Good: The Trials, Tribulations and Triumph of Being...and Staying... a Pittsburgh Pirates Fan Through the '90s and 2000's

Fam-A-Lee First: The Story of the 1979 Pittsburgh Pirates' Remarkable World Series Comeback

Other Sports

Leadoff Hit: Inside the Inaugural Season of the Holly Springs Salamanders

The Hockey Jersey Handbook: A Guide to Collecting and Caring For Jerseys From Throughout the Game

Free Book!

Get the digital version of *Buc to Good: The Trials, Tribulations and Triumph of Being...and Staying... a Pittsburgh Pirates Fan Through the '90s and 2000's* free when you go to my website jasonzemcik.com and subscribe to my newsletter

Everyone knows the story on the surface. The Pittsburgh Pirates suffer a heartbreaking defeat in Game 7 of the 1992 National League Championship Series – the infamous Sid Bream game – and go on to plummet into what became the longest streak of consecutive losing seasons in major professional sports history before finally making it back to the playoffs in dramatic fashion in 2013.

But for the segment of folks who continued to identify themselves as Pirates fans throughout the two-decade journey to redemption, seeing their belief that winning baseball would again be played in Pittsburgh one day come to fruition represents an entirely different story. It's a story of perpetual optimism, of loyalty, and of loving a team like family.

Buc to Good: The Trials, Tribulations and Triumph of Being...and Staying...a Pittsburgh Pirates Fan Through the '90s and 2000's is the story of these fans, as told by one of them. From the low of the '92 NLCS loss, to the "didn't think it could get any worse" years that followed, to the euphoria of the '13 Wild Card Game, *Buc to Good* touches all the bases on each true Pirates fan's emotional ride to seeing their team return to prominence.

CONTENTS

About the Author 3

Also by Jason Zemcik 6

Free Book! 7

Chapter 1 – Because 9

Chapter 2 – A Star from the Start 19

Chapter 3 – A Step Back, and a Leap Forward 31

Chapter 4 – Who Needed Who? 42

Chapter 5 – Better than Everyone's Best…and Worst 52

Chapter 6 – Hockey Was Only Half the Story 63

Chapter 7 – An Unimaginable Save 73

Chapter 8 – Back to the Future 83

Chapter 9 – "See You at Center Ice" 94

One More Thing… 107

Chapter 1 – Because

Because of course he would.

For any other player it would seem too cliché, just too good to be true. But for Mario Lemieux it was, without a doubt, the only appropriate outcome.

Because it's what he'd done time and time again. He made magic, right in front of our very eyes. He made opponents both cry *and* wind their watches, to put a different spin on a classic Mike Lange saying, as he stupefied them with his impeccable sense for being in exactly the right place at the right time and the unworldly ease with which he made the impossible look routine.

Because losing Game 1 of the Stanley Cup Finals on home ice as the defending champions just wasn't an option, even after digging a 4-1 hole midway through the second period against a Chicago Blackhawks team that was firing on all cylinders.

While brilliant play from the entire team helped the Penguins claw their way back into contention during the later stages of that opening game in the 1992 Finals, it was Lemieux that gave the comeback the kind of real, "OK, *now* they're back in it" life that only he could. He notched the third Pittsburgh score by banking in a shot off of Chicago goalie Ed Balfour from behind the goal line to pull the home team to within one as

Chapter 1 – Because

the second period drew to a close. It was the kind of play that, if it came from anyone else, you'd never in a million years believe it was something they meant to do.

He then proceeded to give the Pittsburgh fans one of the most unforgettable moments in the city's sporting history in the final seconds of the game. We can all still picture it as if it were yesterday, though decades have since passed it's still so recent in our minds due to the magnificence that it was made of. With the game tied at 4-4, we all vividly remember Lemieux waiting, lurking, perched in exactly the perfect spot on the doorstep of the Chicago goal and – it's no stretch to say I'm far from alone in this – just knowing what was going to happen.

Because of course the rebound from Penguins' defenseman Larry Murphy's shot would bounce to Balfour's right, directly onto Lemieux's stick as if he knew the precise spot where the puck would be. Positioned perfectly, he slammed it home with 12.6 ticks remaining on the clock, giving the Penguins a 5-4 victory that just an hour earlier seemed more improbable than, well, nothing was really improbable with number 66 on our team. The goal brought the Civic Arena crowd to by many accounts the loudest it had ever been, and made one certain peanut vendor famous for eternity for being in every video clip furiously twirling his hat as the building shook to its decades-old bones from the noise that reverberated through it.

Because one championship simply wasn't enough. Because as that and so many other moments exemplified, Lemieux always saw the game in slow motion, three steps ahead of everyone else on the ice. Because if the year prior chronic back problems and two helpless Minnesota North Stars defenders couldn't stop him, the latter ill-fated attempt coming on another of the most-recognized goals in franchise history, then the 1992 Blackhawks had no chance either.

Fast forward nearly twenty five years later.

The decibel level in the newly-renamed PPG Paints Arena rose from an already loud roar to a deafening mix of applause and top-of-the-lungs cheers from the standing-room-only crowd. Everyone could sense who was next, as the accolades clearly had a different ring to them. It might seem hard to notice a slight variation in tone among thousands of people all screaming at once, but this round was notably unique from the others that seemed to be on a perpetual loop for the duration of the program. These cheers were of a variety that showed their purveyors were well aware of the contribution that the man whose name was next to be called had in making all of what they were currently experiencing possible.

There was no denying that the evening's celebration, raising the Penguins' fourth Stanley Cup banner before the 2016-17 season opener on October 13th, 2016, was for the fans. It was a chance for Penguins supporters, from those who took a short bus ride into the city from any of the outlying

Chapter 1 – Because

communities to those who drove for hours from other states or even flew in from other countries to not miss their chance to celebrate the thrill ride their team had taken them on the previous spring, to see those memories become permanently etched in Pittsburgh hockey history. That pregame ceremony was indeed about every one of the thousands of Penguins fans in attendance and the millions watching or listening from wherever in the world they were.

But it was possible because of him.

Of course that's in many ways an overgeneralized statement. Nothing of the magnitude of winning a Stanley Cup is attributable to one man alone, and it's likely that Lemieux himself would be the first to deflect any credit given to him. But the conditions by which that latest championship, or the Penguins' third that came seven years before it, all became possible?

Now that's a different story.

It is indeed an undeniable truth that both the 2016 Stanley Cup celebration and the overarching situation of franchise stability and steadfastly healthy fan support that had come to mark the Penguins as they embarked upon their 50th anniversary season are the result of one man's staunch commitment to the city of Pittsburgh.

Much to the adoration of the fervent fans, the next name announced as the introductions made their way through the entire Penguins' team and staff, was of course Mario Lemieux. In his typically understated way, the Co-owner and Chairman, a title those of us who grew up watching him dazzle on the ice still can't quite wrap our heads around despite being infinitely thankful for, simply smiled and waved as his name was called. But the pause between his name and the next was a little longer. The television cameras paned in a little closer. Everything about the moment was clearly just a little bit more special, as it absolutely deserved to be.

Because everyone understood without a doubt what his work over the years had meant to the franchise and from a broader perspective, to all of Pittsburgh. Such is the stuff legends are made of, athletes so rare they transcend greatness not only in game performance but in their lasting impact on an organization, a fan base, and a community.

If Mario Lemieux had *only* been a great hockey player his place at the head table of Pittsburgh's larger-than-most-cities' group of sports superstars would be firmly cemented as a multiple-time champion, All Star, and holder of countless records. If he were *only* a generous philanthropist, his charitable efforts having touched the lives of so many cancer patients and their families in the greater Pittsburgh area and beyond, he'd go down as one of the city's most gracious and civic-minded icons ever. And if being an astute businessman was his *only* claim to fame, most notably in salvaging the Penguins from

Chapter 1 – Because

bankruptcy and imminent relocation, he'd still be revered as a local treasure.

But Mario Lemieux has been *all* of those things to the city of Pittsburgh, and in doing so has made a mark that very few sports stars, public figures, or business leaders can match. He's one of a rare breed of athletes whose influence extends far beyond sports, the kind that leaves an indelible impression that spans generations. He's the type of individual whose complete body of work, one that's still ongoing nonetheless, is far greater than brilliance on the stat sheet or even banners hanging from the rafters.

Lemieux's impact on Pittsburgh has given us countless instances to cheer, immeasurable opportunities to beam at one of our own, as he's certainly become over the years, shining both on and off the ice yet doing so in a way that's more modest than one would ever think someone of his accomplishments would be in this day and age of "me first" sports celebrities. His penchant for privacy fascinates us. He's unheard from when his involvement isn't needed, yet front and center when warranted. He's figured this celebrity thing out to an incredible degree, which means there is undoubtedly much of him we'll never figure out.

Knowing about him takes a back seat though to knowing what he's done. For the franchise. For the city. For the fans. Lifting a city on his oft-aching back to make the Penguins as much of a point of local pride as their cross-town sports neighbors who also have a bevy of silver trophies in their own hardware case.

It's almost a story right out of central casting, except for the fact that finding an imaginative and talented enough screenwriter to weave such a tale of magnificence would be a very, very difficult task. The back pain. The surgeries. The cancer diagnosis in the prime of his career. The comeback. Deferring salary payment after payment then stepping up to take ownership of the team rather than stepping into court to simply get his money and, no pun intended, skate away, leaving the franchise with no option but to do the same. We've been fortunate to have witnessed one of the truly great sports figures to ever call Pittsburgh home, and we continue to be among the luckiest fans in all of sports each and every day our team has a guy at the helm committed to doing everything in a first-class manner.

One can argue ad nauseam whether or not Mario Lemieux was the greatest hockey player ever. Simply using career statistics as the barometer, he wasn't, though as we know, numbers hardly tell the entire tale. There's a pretty solid argument for painting him as the most gifted player of all time. Given all of the setbacks that he faced there's little doubt he could have produced career numbers that outpaced everyone else had he had the luxury of playing at even three quarters health for even half of his career.

Chapter 1 – Because

Where there's absolutely zero argument though is in the breadth of Lemieux's holistic impact on Pittsburgh. From delivering not one but two Stanley Cups as a player, making the Penguins a champion after decades as an afterthought in the shadows of the Steelers' Lombardi Trophies and the Pirates' World Series rings, to devoting countless hours, dollars, and amounts of emotional energy to supporting cancer patients and their families through his foundation, to refusing to let the only franchise that he ever played for leave town when the situation was so bleak even a miracle like the ones he delivered on the ice seemed as if it couldn't save the Penguins.

Because that's Mario Lemieux. His career, his evolution from player to owner, and all of his philanthropic work in between have all been touched with an air of greatness, a flavor of excellence and above all, commitment to Pittsburgh that simply can't be matched.

For those of us who were fortunate to have just taken an interest in hockey as he was coming into the prime of his career he was the impetus for a lifelong devotion to our team, the guy who made hockey matter to so many and who ignited an entire generation of Penguins fans that are now bringing up another generation. If he hadn't landed in Pittsburgh, one can only wonder what would have been. Actually, there's no need to wonder, as hockey, in any form much less the one we've come to know it, wouldn't be a part of the Pittsburgh sports equation.

As fans we're always greedy. There's no denying it, and anyone who does is flat out lying to themselves. Our team wins a championship, which is infinitely hard to do in any sport at any level, and we celebrate it for a short while before turning our focus to wanting two. Win two and we want three. Claim a scoring title and we want an MVP award to go with it. We're always looking for more, and in that sense so many of us feel that we got robbed by not getting to see Lemieux's magnificence to its full extent throughout a career that was undoubtedly cut short by injuries.

And nothing could be more ridiculous, more laughable, more downright selfish of us. Because robbed is the last thing that we were when it came to Lemieux's playing career. We had the good fortune of seeing quite possibly the greatest player ever in terms of pure skill wear our jersey and only our jersey across a twenty-plus year span of time. There were interruptions along the way, breaks in the action, but how many fans of other teams would gladly take just one year of having such a talent on their roster?

The Penguins are in Pittsburgh to stay. The Pittsburgh we now know is here to stay, and let that sink in for just a moment as it's no secret that the multitude of hospitals and associated endowments and fellowships and research grants that gave

Chapter 1 – Because

rise to so many other opportunities for revitalization in the post-steel era didn't just materialize out of thin air.

We clearly were the lucky ones. We still are.

I don't personally know Mario Lemieux. I've never met him, let alone had the opportunity to get any sort of "behind the scenes" look into his world that, from most accounts, is reserved for a small circle of individuals he keeps close. I'm simply a hockey fan who grew up as his career progressed, and marveled at not only his skill and resilience on the ice but also his steadfast commitment to the Penguins and Pittsburgh.

What I do know is simply what I've seen firsthand – the evolution of both the team and the city over the preceding three decades and his influence on each. This book is simply an account of my own appreciation for what he has done, a sentiment that I undoubtedly share with so many Pittsburghers. And while there have certainly been a host of other cursory factors involved in everything that has transpired during the Lemieux era, it's by no means a stretch to say that it all came about *because* of one guy.

Chapter 2 – A Star from the Start

Pete Peeters was a darn good NHL goalie. He won just shy of 250 games over 13 seasons and was a four-time All Star. He even won the Veznia Trophy as the best netminder in the league in 1983. Similarly, his Boston Bruins teammate Ray Bourque was, at the time, entering the fifth season of what would be a Hall of Fame career. An All Star every season since entering the NHL, Bourque had firmly established himself as one of the best defensemen in the game.

Neither player was a slouch by any stretch, yet both of them looked as helpless as bantam players on that night, October 11th, 1984. Just moments after the national anthem and with plenty of fans in the Boston Garden still settling into their seats for what was the opening game of the season for both teams, the premier act in a career that would go on to be one of the greatest ever known to hockey, and all of sports, took place.

The Penguins tried to clear the puck from their own zone in four-on-four action early in the first period, but Boston's Bourque kept the play alive by snagging it along the boards just inside the blue line. Almost instantaneously though, the Penguins' highly-touted rookie phenom swooped in and pickpocketed Bourque. Off to the races with only open ice and Peeters ahead of him, Lemieux showed for the first time

Chapter 2 – A Star from the Start

one of the signature moves that he quickly became known for and that youth hockey players would soon be emulating on rinks, ponds, and driveways around the world.

He crossed over to his backhand, drawing Peeters out of position before flipping the puck past him, scoring his first NHL goal on his very first shot, less than three minutes into his career. The Penguins' bench erupted with excitement while Lemieux displayed a smile and energetic fist pump as his teammates congratulated him on the ice and one of his fellow rookies, defenseman Doug Bodger, retrieved the puck to preserve the historic moment. The Mario Lemieux era in Pittsburgh had officially arrived, and in grand fashion.

Lost in the excitement of the highlight reel goal was the fact that earlier in the same shift Lemieux had also showcased his lethal forechecking ability, swiping the puck from Bruins' defender Mats Thelin behind the Boston goal and feeding Penguins' winger Rick Kehoe for a scoring opportunity in the slot. Even a 4-3 loss when the game was over couldn't quell the excitement of the entire Pittsburgh organization and its fan base, what existed of it that is. In a town where the Steelers and Pirates were both only five years removed from winning championships, the Penguins were largely an afterthought to many.

The 19-year old Lemieux, selected as the first overall pick in the NHL draft the summer prior, was to be their savior. The unworldly talent that would resurrect a franchise that many questioned the viability of given its unimpressive to moderate at best record on the ice and sparse showing at the gate during its history. A heavy burden for sure, but as he showed in his debut, if anyone was up to it he was Pittsburgh's man.

Six nights later the hometown fans got their first glimpse of their new star when the Penguins opened the home portion of their schedule against the Vancouver Canucks. Not only did Lemieux set up an early goal in the win, the club's first of the season, he also surprised many including his own teammates when he dropped his gloves to fight Vancouver's Gary Lupul just over two minutes into the first period. With a significant height advantage, Lemieux landed blow after blow until Vancouver goalie John Garrett came to Lupul's rescue, rushing into the fray to help his teammate fend off Lemieux before the officials took control. Beyond winning the fight, Lemieux quickly won over the Pittsburgh fans. His early display of determination clearly set the tone for things to come in his tenure with the Penguins.

At that season's All Star Game in Calgary, Lemieux cemented himself as the game's brightest young star in front of a league-wide audience. His first All Star goal came with an ironic twist, as one of the assisting players was none other than Bourque, whom he had stolen the puck from in scoring his first career goal months prior. Bourque centered a pass in the slot to the New Jersey Devils' Kirk Muller that Muller dropped neatly back to a streaking Lemieux, who sniped a

Chapter 2 – A Star from the Start

close range shot past goalie Grant Fuhr of the Edmonton Oilers.

Lemieux's second goal of the game also had its own bit of irony. It came on a strong rush up the boards, as he muscled his way through the Campbell Conference defenders and in on Fuhr for another close range shot just one minute of game action after Edmonton's Wayne Gretzky, largely regarded as the best player in the game and thus the standard by which Lemieux was already being judged as a teenager, had scored. For the player who would later grace a Sports Illustrated cover with the headline asking *"As Great as Gretzky?"* it was almost an "anything you can do I can do better" moment from Lemieux.

That goal proved to be the game winner for the Wales Conference. For his performance Lemieux was named the game MVP, the first rookie to earn the accolade. The rest of his initial campaign brought continued success. On the season Lemieux finished with an even 100 points and was awarded the Calder Trophy as Rookie of the Year, hardly a surprise to anyone who watched him play. He had indeed lived up to his billing, showing his dazzling stickhandling ability, superior strength, almost magical touch, and ability to create offense that rivaled any player in the game.

It was as if the Pittsburgh fan base was so excited by Lemieux's success that they failed to realize, or rather weren't bothered by, the fact that the Penguins' team results didn't immediately follow suit.

There were a few bright spots – a five game winning streak in December and an undefeated record in overtime games on the year to name a few. But the season had far more negatives, including a stretch of twelve winless games, eleven losses and a tie, in January and February that officially sunk any scant hope the team had of sneaking into the Patrick Division playoff race. Lemieux's magnificent scoring numbers had a damper put on them by one other figure that spoke volumes in its contrast, his minus 35 overall rating. It was glaring indicator that the Penguins clearly had work to do in assembling a supporting cast around their new star.

While Lemieux didn't bring an immediate transformation in the wins and losses department that first season, his performance did account for something just as valuable, if not more. He brought hope, and an abundance of it to be exact. The Pittsburgh fans finally had the franchise player they could envision leading them to the Stanley Cup years down the road, even if at the time just becoming a legitimate playoff contender was going to be no small task.

The following season saw Lemieux increase his scoring numbers in all categories, finishing with 141 points and second in the voting for the Hart Memorial Trophy as league Most Valuable Player. In addition, he took home the Lester B. Pearson award as the most outstanding player in the regular

Chapter 2 – A Star from the Start

season and was again named to the Wales Conference All Star team.

Beyond Lemieux's individual improvement, the 1985-86 season brought a 10-win increase for the Penguins. They still finished four games under the .500 mark however. The also missed out on the fourth and final postseason spot in the Patrick Division by two points despite defeating the New York Rangers, the team they were battling for the fourth-place position, 5-4 in overtime at Madison Square Garden on the final day of the regular season and holding the head-to-head tiebreaker against New York which would have come into play the two teams finished deadlocked. Despite the disappointment of narrowly missing the playoffs, the season was far from a failure. The 10-win improvement represented the franchise's largest season-over-season increase since the 1978-79 campaign, a positive sign that with their new star, the Penguins were indeed heading in the right direction.

The following season brought about a bit of a hiccup in Lemieux's early success and in turn, the Penguins' upward trend. Despite remaining relatively healthy during his first two years in the NHL, and even playing in all but one of the Penguins' contests in the year prior, Lemieux missed 17 games during the 1986-87 campaign due to a knee injury and a bout with bronchitis, though he still put up impressive individual statistics. He again led the Penguins in goals, assists, and total points, and his 54 goal output was good for third in the NHL.

He was also named an All Star for the third time in his three seasons, though the annual game between NHL conferences was replaced by Rendez-vous '87, a two-game exhibition held in Quebec between the NHL All Stars and the Soviet National Team.

The event gave Lemieux an opportunity to shine on an international stage, and shine he did. The teams eschewed the traditionally relaxed pace of play common to the All Star Game as international bragging rights were on the line, and Lemieux delivered in the clutch for the NHL squad in the first game. Tied 3-3 and approaching the final minute of regulation, Lemieux skated into the Soviet zone with the puck and snapped a wrist shot from between the faceoff circles that slipped by goaltender Yevgeni Belosheikin to put the NHL in the lead. Replays showed that NHL teammate and Patrick Division rival Dave Poulin of the Philadelphia Flyers got a stick on Lemieux's shot and redirected it just in front of the goal crease. Poulin was ultimately credited with the score, though Lemieux's impact on the NHL team's impactful win was clearly felt in his late-game effort.

In 1987-88 Lemieux was again named an All Star, and delivered a stirring performance in St. Louis when the midseason inter-NHL contest resumed. He notched an All Star Game record six points, including the game winning goal in overtime. On the season Lemieux took home a hat trick of awards for his brilliant play. He earned his first career Art

Chapter 2 – A Star from the Start

Ross Trophy as the league's leading scorer as his 168 points dethroned Gretzky after a seven year run. In addition he also claimed the Hart Trophy as well as his second Pearson award as the most outstanding player in the regular season.

Those two words however – regular season – called to mind the glaring void in Lemieux's tenure in Pittsburgh to that point. Though the Penguins increased their win total from the previous season by six, their point total by nine, and finished one game above .500, their first winning season since 1978-79, they again finished on the outside of the playoff race looking in.

Through four seasons the Penguins had yet to parlay their acquisition of Lemieux into a postseason berth, something that was not lost on anyone. Therein lied the crux of the early Lemieux years in Pittsburgh. He proved without a doubt to be everything he was advertised to be when the Penguins stumbled to their pitiful 16-win season in 1983-84 and earned the right to draft him, but his tremendous individual talent had yet to translate into significant team success.

In the 1988-89 campaign that began to change. After again dazzling on the world stage over the offseason, this time in pairing with Gretzky to lead Team Canada's victory in the Canada Cup in what amounted to a true coming of age experience for Lemieux, he reached another level in his already brilliant play during the NHL season. He posted 85 goals and 199 points for the year, good for his second consecutive scoring title.

He scored almost at will – literally, in some cases, such as in his New Year's Eve 1988 gem that will forever remain one of the most remarkable single game performances in NHL history. Lemieux netted five goals against the New Jersey Devils that night, one each way possible – even strength, shorthanded, on the power play, via a penalty shot, and into an empty net. The Penguins' winning percentage shot up as well, as they finished second in the Patrick Division and finally earned their first playoff spot since the 1981-82 season.

Leading his Penguins, as they had clearly become, to the postseason for the first time was yet another step in Lemieux's maturation as a team leader and premier NHL star. The Penguins swept the New York Rangers in the opening round where he scored in three of the four Pittsburgh victories. The Patrick Division finals against the cross-state rival Flyers did not end as well though, despite even more outstanding play by Lemieux. The Penguins dropped the series in seven games, though Lemieux registered nine goals including a five-score performance on home ice in Game 5. He also scored the lone Pittsburgh goal in the Penguins' 4-1 Game 7 defeat. While the year ended in disappointment, it represented another stepping stone in the eyes of the Penguins' faithful, the continuance of a process by which Lemieux was pulling them out of hockey irrelevance.

Chapter 2 – A Star from the Start

The following year appeared ripe for the Penguins to continue their maturation into a bona fide contender in the Wales Conference. Lemieux didn't disappoint, hovering near the league lead in scoring throughout the early part of the schedule. The Penguins as a team were consistently chasing the .500 mark, managing to stay just a few games back but well in contention for a second straight playoff berth.

Pittsburgh played host to the All Star Game that year, and Lemieux stole the show in front of the home fans like only he could. The excitement was bubbling over before the puck dropped, as the Pittsburgh Civic Arena crowd began its standing ovation for Lemieux well before he was announced during the pregame introductions. Just twenty one seconds into the game Lemieux scored his first goal of the afternoon and didn't look back, notching a first period hat trick on his way to a four-goal outing and another All Star Game MVP award.

His host of goals in that game showcased the multitude of varieties in which his lethality came. On the first he used his unworldly reach to wrap the puck past Campbell Conference goaltender Mike Vernon of the Calgary Flames. His second was a blistering slap shot from just inside the blue line that beat Vernon through the five hole. And while those two scores may have been merely routine plays for Lemieux, his third goal was pure magnificence by any barometer. He took a lead pass from Pittsburgh teammate Paul Coffey and after gaining the offensive zone, executed a toe drag as drawn out as a lazy southern Sunday afternoon. Lemieux artfully controlled the puck, waiting for the precise moment that Chicago's Doug Wilson committed to trying to swipe it away before crossing over and literally making him fall down on the seat of his pants before crossing up Vernon in similar fashion to deposit the puck into a nearly empty net. That game, a 12-7 Wales Conference victory once all was said and done, was largely representative of the early Lemieux years in Pittsburgh. If the hometown fans ever thought they had seen the full extent of his brilliance, he found another way after another way to dazzle them with his artistry on ice.

The excitement that had taken hold in the Steel City thanks to Lemieux was indeed palpable, as his dazzling display in front of Pittsburgh's All Star crowd only confirmed. The fans clearly recognized that he was the NHL's premier young star and, in a time when the Steelers and Pirates were further removed from their championships of the late 1970's and each presently going through down spells, were anxiously anticipating the team's successes increasing in parallel with his individual accomplishments. With just over two months remaining in the season the Penguins were positioned to again qualify for the Stanley Cup playoffs and had hopes of advancing even deeper than they had in the previous year's run.

Chapter 2 – A Star from the Start

Lemieux also built up a 35-game scoring streak that, similar to a pitcher carrying a no hitter into the later innings of a baseball game, was beginning to garner widespread attention as it drew closer to Gretzky's NHL record of 51 games. Times were indeed good on the ice in Pittsburgh, but indicative of a theme that unfortunately would plague Lemieux and as a result the Penguins throughout his career, they were about to hit a difficult patch in the weeks ahead.

Chapter 3 – A Step Back, and a Leap Forward

When, as the story goes, you team up with your brothers one childhood night to lock your babysitter in a room so you can watch hockey instead of what she had planned for the evening, you're not exactly one to give up easily when it comes to anything dealing with the sport. When that thing happens to be your months-long chase of the longest scoring streak in NHL history, that reluctance grows even more pronounced.

At the time I was eight years old, and over the preceding few weeks had become largely consumed by hockey and more specifically, Lemieux. A few weeks after spending a Sunday afternoon marveling at the All Star scoring clinic he put on, I came home from school and settled in for a Valentine's Day evening showdown as the Penguins took the ice against the Rangers at Madison Square Garden.

I was, like so many other Pittsburgh fans of all ages, fascinated by the idea that my team had one of the best players in the game and that he happened to be chasing a pretty significant record. But part of the early summary I had gathered on Lemieux when I first started watching hockey included his struggles with back problems throughout his career, so when the moment arrived in that game it wasn't without prefacing. I remember the feeling of disappointment upon finding out as the third period commenced that Super Mario, as he had

Chapter 3 – A Step Back, and a Leap Forward

affectionately become known among the Pittsburgh fans, was finally giving up the remarkable streak.

Lemieux remained in the training room when play resumed, unable to again take the ice after having being held scoreless as he struggled through the game's first forty minutes. Even though I was relatively new to following the Penguins, Lemieux's constant battle with injury was well documented. Few in Pittsburgh hadn't heard the stories detailing nights when his back pain was so severe he needed help to simply lace up his skates. On that particular night it finally, and very begrudgingly, got the best of him.

The babysitter anecdote being a humorous example among the multitudes of serious ones from his play since entering the league, Lemieux's determination was clearly a thing that didn't break easily. The injury led him to miss the next several weeks of play. Sitting out the remainder of the season was undoubtedly not the way that anyone envisioned the campaign coming to a close, but on a larger scale it wasn't what anyone imagined or wanted for Lemieux as he was coming fully into the prime of his career.

Without him the Penguins stumbled down the stretch, managing only five wins over the season's final month and a half. Lemieux showed his grit and determination in the season's final game though, as with the Penguins still in contention for a playoff berth he suited up to play. Although he hadn't seen game action in over a month he managed to score a goal, but it wasn't enough. The Penguins fell to the Buffalo Sabres in overtime to once again finish on the outside of the playoff picture looking in. It was a disappointment for sure after being a win away from the conference finals the year prior, but nothing to the degree of the news that would break that offseason.

By early July Lemieux's back pain had worsened to the extent that the Penguins' medical staff deemed surgery a necessity. It was later revealed that the team and Lemieux had discussed surgery as an option earlier in the season but he had fittingly opted to forego it in hopes of continuing to play through his ailments. A badly herniated disc finally brought the condition to a tipping point, leading Lemieux to undergo the procedure. There was cutting and bone shaving and all the things involved that would make anyone cringe and wonder about their physical future even if their job didn't involve taking bruising NHL checks or trying to contort their body in a multitude of ways to sidestep and bypass defenders night in and night out.

There were also the disconcerting thoughts of what would happen if the operation didn't cure his ailments and enable him to return to world-class form. At only 24 years of age Lemieux was at the top of his game and was supposed to have many more years of brilliance ahead of him. The Penguins' offseason plans, which included hiring USA Hockey President Bob Johnson as their new head coach less than a month prior

Chapter 3 – A Step Back, and a Leap Forward

and adding Bryan Trottier, a four-time Stanley Cup champion with the New York Islanders, to bolster the club with a veteran presence just a few days after Lemieux went under the knife, could potentially be rendered moot by their cornerstone not being available for the coming season. A worst-case scenario, the thought of the surgery solving one problem but causing another more serious one, also entered the minds of many.

Osteomyelitis isn't a household term, but it became one in Pittsburgh as the Penguins headed to training camp in the fall of 1990. News broke that Lemieux had developed the condition – a bone infection which in his case had presented itself in the portion of his spine near where the surgery was performed – and would miss the start of the season with no particular timetable for a return. It was the type of complication that could very well impact Lemieux's health from a long-term well-being standpoint, not simply a hockey one.

Despite the grim news, the Penguins remained cautiously optimistic that Lemieux could make a return that season, though exactly when, and in what form, remained very much up in the air. His teammates held serve admirably during his absence. Wingers Mark Recchi and Kevin Stevens carried the scoring load while a rookie from Czechoslovakia (now the Czech Republic) named Jaromir Jagr also proved to be a formidable scoring threat. The 1990 portion of the schedule came and went without Lemieux seeing game action as did the majority of January when 1991 arrived.

On January 26th however, over halfway through the season, the welcome sight of Lemieux's number 66 sweater hanging in the Penguins' dressing room was finally seen again when the team travelled to the Colisée de Québec to face the Nordiques. Just a few hours up the St. Lawrence River from his native Ville-Émard neighborhood in Montreal, Lemieux wasted no time making his presence felt in his return to the ice. He didn't register a goal but assisted on three Pittsburgh scores in a 6-5 win. Two nights later he made his season debut in front of the home fans, notching a goal and an assist to help the Penguins outpace their Patrick Division rivals the Washington Capitals.

Healthy was a relative term considering the long term impact of his back ailments, a condition that Lemieux and the Penguins' medical staff realized would never return to its pre-aggravated state and could only be managed as best as possible going forward. But given where he was less than twelve months prior it was entirely reasonable to say that being back on the ice and contributing to the Penguins' playoff push for the second half of the season represented a tremendous victory.

Hanging in third place in the Patrick Division as March commenced, the Penguins' brass made the move that not only solidified its commitment to building a winner around

Lemieux and forcing their way into the playoff picture, but that also set the stage, unbeknownst to many yet likely largely predictable to some, for the future of Penguins hockey and Lemieux's lasting impact on it. In a trade deadline deal the Penguins sent forward John Cullen and defenseman Zarley Zalapski to the Hartford Whalers in exchange for center and future Hall of Famer Ron Francis and defensemen Ulf Samuelsson and Grant Jennings.

The deal made waves in Pittsburgh for its tremendous risk. At the time Cullen was an up and coming talent with a seemingly bright future that many weren't happy to see offloaded. The move quickly showed its potential reward though. Francis caught stride in black and gold, bolstering the Penguins' already-potent scoring punch, while Samuelsson fit perfectly into the role of Lemieux's bodyguard, a position that undoubtedly would become critical for Pittsburgh to make a strong postseason push.

The Penguins captured their first-ever division title by closing the season with a 9-4-2 month of March that included a dramatic 5-4 overtime victory at home against the Rangers, the team they were battling for the top spot. Just days later they notched the title-clinching victory on the road in Detroit, and in the process furthered the legitimate belief among fans that they finally had the pieces in place around their superstar to make a run at postseason glory.

The Penguins drew New Jersey in the opening round of the playoffs, a club that they had played fairly even during the regular season by beating four times out of seven matchups. The Devils came into the series with a clear plan to try and bruise and batter Lemieux into being a non-factor. He scored the opening goal of Game 1, but the Devils rallied for two third period goals to steal the opener at the Civic Arena and with it, home ice advantage for the series. Game 2 saw more of the same physical play from New Jersey but the Penguins prevailed in overtime on a brilliant Jagr goal that became all-time Penguins highlight reel material in its own right. Lemieux had two assists in the contest, and the Penguins appeared to be back on track as the series shifted to the Meadowlands for Games 3 and 4.

Pittsburgh won Game 3 to regain the series advantage, but the Devils rebounded to win Game 4 at home to even the series. They then held Lemieux scoreless as they stole Game 5 in Pittsburgh, putting the Penguins in an elimination situation heading back to New Jersey for Game 6. Further complicating matters for the Penguins was the fact that starting goaltender Tom Barrasso was sidelined with an injury, pressing backup Frank Pietrangelo into action for the critical contest.

Pietrangelo was up to the task though, and made one of the most brilliant and best remembered saves in NHL playoff history when he robbed New Jersey's Peter Stastny from point

Chapter 3 – A Step Back, and a Leap Forward

blank range to preserve a Penguins' lead and ultimately force a decisive Game 7. The Penguins carried the momentum of their Game 6 road victory into the series finale in Pittsburgh and never looked back. Pietrangelo remained on fire and Lemieux netted a goal as the Penguins blanked New Jersey 4-0 to claim the series and set up a date with the Capitals in the Patrick Division finals

Though they again dropped the series opener on home ice, the matchup against the Capitals proved to be less difficult for the Penguins to navigate. Pittsburgh rebounded to win the next four games including two on the road to claim a 4-1 series victory and punch their ticket to the Wales Conference Finals for the first time in franchise history. For the series Lemieux registered just two goals but assisted on seven others, clearly showing his danger not just as a scoring threat but as a creator of offensive opportunities for his teammates.

The Penguins faced Boston in the Conference Finals, a franchise that, in contrast to Pittsburgh, was no stranger to postseason glory. The Bruins had at the time won five Stanley Cups in their storied history, and the 1990-91 edition of the team was looking to return to the Finals after falling to the Oilers the year prior. Through the first two games of the series, played at the famed Boston Garden, it looked as if the Bruins' experience and mystique would be too much for the Penguins to overcome.

Boston won the series opener 6-3 behind two goals from their own star, Cam Neely, and held on to also claim Game 2 by a tally of 5-4 despite Lemieux notching two goals and an assist for the Penguins. Though the first two games did little to dispel the notion many outside of Pittsburgh held that the Bruins' aura was simply too much for the Penguins to overcome, when the series shifted back to the Civic Arena it took a turn sharper than if it were heading down the Allegheny and quickly pivoted back up the Monongahela.

Stevens got the Penguins off and running with the opening goal of Game 3 after declaring in one of the off day media sessions that the Penguins would indeed win the series. Lemieux notched a goal that was a brilliant display of his sheer power as he thwarted a developing Boston rush by stealing the puck at the blue line then charging in on goal to beat Bruins' netminder Andy Moog from close range, as well as an assist as the Penguins won 4-1 to cut the series deficit in half.

Two nights later Pittsburgh defeated Boston by the same 4-1 margin with Lemieux again contributing a goal and an assist. With the series tied, the Penguins looked dramatically different from the team that had dropped the first two contests in Boston and had been written off by many as not yet ready for the true pressure cooker that the later rounds of the Stanley Cup playoffs brought. Clearly the pendulum of momentum in the series had swung in the Penguins' favor as they headed back on the road.

Chapter 3 – A Step Back, and a Leap Forward

The Penguins parlayed that momentum into a dominant 7-2 Game 5 victory in Boston. Lemieux found the back of the net and perhaps even more importantly, assisted on three other Pittsburgh goals for a total of four points. The Penguins had clearly shattered the Garden mystique to come to within one victory of earning the franchise's first ever Stanley Cup Finals berth.

Two nights later in front of a capacity Civic Arena crowd that included many who had been waiting decades to see their Penguins do just that, they delivered. Ahead 4-3 as the game's final minute ticked away and facing an extra Bruins' attacker, Lemieux put the game out of reach for good as he lifted a wrist shot from alongside the boards just on the opposite side of center ice that landed perfectly in the Boston goal to set the final score at 5-3 Pittsburgh.

On the series Lemieux torched the Bruins for six goals and 15 total points, proving once again that he was up to the task of fighting through every opponent's attempts to stifle his playmaking ability and derail his pursuit of hockey's biggest prize. At the postgame trophy presentation Lemieux broke with superstition in a major way. He not only touched the Prince of Wales Trophy despite the staunch refusal by many team captains to do so as an indication of the Stanley Cup being the only trophy their club had visions of holding, but he also went as far as to skate it around the Civic Arena ice. It was, clearly, a nod to the loyalty of the long-awaiting

Pittsburgh fans. A show of what the Penguins had finally accomplished after all their years of futility prior to his arrival and the longer than desired wait to finally get to the postseason in his first few campaigns.

But there was one more river to cross, figuratively speaking, for the team that represented the city famous for three of them, and led by the player who grew up not far from the banks of one of Canada's mightiest. One more step to permanently etch their names in hockey history and one more rung for Lemieux to climb in his ascent to the pinnacle of the sport. And, in fitting fashion, he would deliver a performance for the ages in the process – one that left no doubt about his ability to perform on the game's grandest stage and against the toughest of adversity.

Chapter 4 – Who Needed Who?

The Penguins didn't just need it, all of Pittsburgh did.

Having recently surpassed a decade since the last time a black and gold team culminated its season with a championship, the threat of falling back among the sporting masses was slowly beginning to creep in. The Steelers' dynasty had catapulted Pittsburgh into elite company, and in 1979 it became only the fourth city to win two major professional sports in the same year when the Pirates got in on the party with their fifth World Series triumph. But after the Steelers capped their run of four championships in six seasons, Pittsburgh entered a dry spell that spanned the rest of the 1980's. While it would never go away, the strength of the city's championship pride was starting to fade ever so slightly by the time 1991 arrived.

With the Steelers at that time mired in a stretch in which they made the playoffs in only one of six seasons and the Pirates having won a division title the previous year only to fall to the Cincinnati Reds in the National League Championship Series, Pittsburgh was longing for another champion to again return it to sporting prominence. And the Penguins, needless to say, were still in search of a title to fully legitimize the franchise. For all that bringing on Lemieux had done in the name of churning up interest and fueling attendance and brightening the future, one fact remained very clear. The Penguins had never won a championship.

Along with that factual assessment came the obvious corollary. Lemieux, he of All Star Game greatness and scoring prowess and most recently an inspiring comeback from a potentially devastating injury, also had yet to hoist the Stanley Cup. Now seven seasons into his career, and despite having led his native Canada to victory in the Canada Cup against a field of the world's best players, he had yet to place his hands on the most recognized trophy in all of sports, the one that defined so many players' careers.

Thus when Game 1 of the 1991 Stanley Cup Finals came to the Civic Arena on May 15th, along with it for Lemieux came the opportunity for coronation of sorts. A forum to show hockey fans everywhere that he was not only the most dominant player in the game but also the bedrock of a championship squad. And though the stage was set, the Penguins' opponent in those finals, the upstart Minnesota North Stars, had other ideas.

Despite finishing the regular season with a record below .500, the North Stars qualified for playoffs by virtue of claiming the fourth spot in the Norris Division. Once the postseason commenced though, a different Minnesota club emerged. The North Stars knocked off the Chicago Blackhawks, Presidents' Trophy winners as the league's best regular season team, in six games. They followed up that remarkable feat by

Chapter 4 – Who Needed Who?

eliminating the league's second-best regular season team, the St. Louis Blues, in the Norris Division Finals also by a tally of four games to two. The magical ride didn't end there, as in the Campbell Conference Finals Minnesota defeated the defending champion Oilers 4-1 to earn a most unlikely Stanley Cup Finals berth.

Many hockey pundits were beginning to believe the North Stars were a team of destiny, and their performance in Game 1 only amplified that belief. Though the Penguins got on the board first and Lemieux scored shorthanded in the second period, Minnesota methodically scratched out a 5-4 victory to steal home ice advantage. While not the start anyone in black and gold had hoped for, it wasn't overly concerning given the Penguins' losses in each of the series openers that had preceded it. It did, however, set up what was as close to a must-win situation as could be in Game 2, as it wasn't lost on anyone that going back to Minnesota down 0-2 against a team as hot as the North Stars would be ill-advised to say the least.

The Penguins responded in kind. They got a shorthanded goal from winger Bob Errey to open the scoring and then a power play goal from Stevens, with an assist from Lemieux, to take a 2-0 lead into the first intermission. Minnesota climbed right back into the contest in the first minute of the second period on a Mike Modano power play tally, which set the conditions for one of the most remarkable moments in NHL history, courtesy of none other than Lemieux.

It is a goal that to this day ranks among the most brilliant the game has ever seen. For those who didn't have the good fortune to experience it when it happened, either in person or on television, the NHL highlight reels have maintained it for eternity, as well they should. It's a moment that bears preserving for future generations as one of the most remarkable displays of individual hockey skill ever.

In the context of when it took place, with his team down a game in the Stanley Cup Finals and holding a tenuous lead in a tightly-contested Game 2, it was even more impressive. With just over five minutes remaining in the second period Lemieux took a breakout pass near center ice, splitting two Minnesota defenders and slipping the puck between the legs of one, Shawn Chambers, before barreling in on goaltender Jon Casey and making one of his signature crossover moves to score the goal that put the game firmly in the Penguins' grasp. As the Civic Arena crowd erupted, Lange punctuated the moment with one of his greatest calls of all time, beaming "He left 'em on the Parkway goin' to the airport!" The goal propelled the Penguins to a 4-1 victory, evening the series as it headed to Minnesota.

But despite the inspiring performance in Pittsburgh two nights before, the Penguins faced another setback when the venue shifted to Minneapolis for Game 3. Lemieux was scratched from the lineup, his back flaring up again to the point that it rendered him unable to play even given the

Chapter 4 – Who Needed Who?

importance of the situation and his every effort to make a go of it.

Minnesota sensed the opportunity at hand and jumped on it, scoring two second period goals within a minute of each other to open up a lead after the teams had battled scoreless for the game's first 27 minutes. The Penguins made a valiant attempt to fight their way back into the contest without Lemieux, getting a third period goal from Phil Bourque that cut the deficit to 2-1, but it wasn't enough. Minnesota claimed the victory by a final tally of 3-1 and retook the series lead.

While the loss again placed the Penguins in a difficult, though not dire, situation, the more pressing concern was whether Lemieux would be back on the ice 48 hours later when the puck dropped for Game 4. To the relief of every Penguins fan he was, and his presence energized Pittsburgh to come storming back after the Game 3 defeat. The Penguins erupted for three goals in the first five minutes of the contest, one of them from Lemieux, and held off a late Minnesota comeback attempt to claim a 5-3 victory and even the series at 2-2 going back to Pittsburgh.

In front of the home crowd Lemieux again seized the moment, leading another Penguins' early-game outburst in Game 5 that had the Civic Arena crowd alive with visions of the city's first Stanley Cup that were ever so closer to becoming reality.

If his Game 2 gem wasn't enough Lemieux notched another highlight reel goal to open the scoring for Pittsburgh, banking in a shot from behind the goal line off of Casey. He also assisted on two Recchi scores as the Penguins skated out to a 4-0 lead through the first 14 minutes. Minnesota again mounted a comeback, but again it wasn't enough. When the final horn sounded, the scoreboard showing a 6-4 Pittsburgh victory, only 60 minutes of hockey stood between the Penguins and their first Stanley Cup.

While so many were understandably caught up in the excitement, the victory offered many long-suffering Penguins fans a sort of "moment before the moment" to reflect on all that had transpired to bring their team to the point it was at. All of the bad years. All of the anticipation throughout the 1983-84 season about where they'd finish in the standings and consequently what their draft position would be knowing that a once-in-a-generation talent like Lemieux awaited. All of the patience, or was it impatience, during the first few seasons as the Penguins assembled a winner around him. All of the injury concerns, the missed games, all of the opponents' attempts to physically inhibit Lemieux's drive to bring Pittsburgh to the top of the hockey mountain. All of those thoughts danced through the minds of many as their Penguins sat on the brink of finally becoming champions, with the opportunity to close the deal when the series moved back to Minneapolis.

Chapter 4 – Who Needed Who?

The Penguins not only seized that opportunity, they grasped it with a stranglehold that clearly, emphatically, showed they weren't about to let it slip by. Despite an impassioned Met Center crowd that did everything it could to will the North Stars to victory and the chance to play one more game for all the marbles, the Penguins were simply no match. Samuelsson opened the scoring just two minutes into the game with a power play tally, and Lemieux followed with a breakaway score where he again crossed up Casey in an astonishing display of stick work.

It's as if that Lemieux goal was a signal to the Penguins to open the flood gates, and the rest of the game was quite literally all Pittsburgh. The Penguins routed the North Stars 8-0 to complete the franchise's transformation from doormat to champion, and Lange celebrated the final moment with another of his game calls that will live for eternity in the minds of all Pittsburgh fans, saying "The Stanley Cup has come to the city of Pittsburgh!"

All told, Lemieux bested two opponents in that Finals matchup – the North Stars' defense of course and also his ever-present back issues, which by the time his season, even shortened as it was, reached May had again proved to be a significant hurdle for him to overcome. But overcome he did, and in the process he staked his own claim as the game's preeminent superstar. His 44 points in 23 playoff games were more than just a bevy of timely goals and assists, more than

Legacy of Excellence

just momentum swings and shows of grit and determination and leadership all rolled into one. They were a representation of Lemieux holding up his end of the deal as the franchise's cornerstone, something that anyone who had the gift of immense foresight would have realized would become a recurring theme in Pittsburgh over the years to come.

Lemieux scored and created and dazzled, and when he wasn't doing any of that he was a diversion, which was just as valuable to the Penguins' game plan. Simply put, during that 1991 Stanley Cup run he was all of the things he was brought to town to be. Ultimately he was simply the best player on a team that was bound and determined to win a championship for a city that was once again hungry, overdue even, for one. Those eight weeks and 24 games in the spring of 1991 were a ride that not only bound the Penguins to Pittsburgh in a "finally part of the championship club" sense, but also put the city on top again for the rest of the world to see.

Pittsburgh needed all of that, and it got it thanks in no small part to Lemieux. Did he win the Stanley Cup that year all by himself? Absolutely not. Could the Penguins have won it without him? It's safe to say we all know the answer to that. Seeing Lemieux hoist the Conn Smythe Trophy as playoff MVP after making his skate with the Cup just confirmed it. He was unequivocally the key piece in the championship puzzle, the captain of the ship on the route to accomplishing what then General Manager Eddie Johnston envisioned for

Chapter 4 – Who Needed Who?

the team's future when making the Penguins' selection in the 1984 draft.

But more than just giving Pittsburgh what it needed, winning the Stanley Cup represented a milestone for Lemieux equally as much in getting what he needed from the ardent fans and proud city. By finally leading his team to the Cup he had ascended to all-time superstar status – a rite of passage of sorts, a seat at the table among other NHL greats. For whatever the sport, and regardless of the other personal stat lines and accomplishments that are part of the equation, elite players are, for better or worse, largely viewed through the lens of championships. Lemieux was now part of that club, and the fact that his evolution, his maturation into not only a dominant player but also the unquestioned leader of a team, even given the setbacks he had faced, was helped considerably by playing in a city that offered the right environment for him to flourish wasn't lost on anyone.

The Pittsburgh fans had proven to be the right base to support him but also to let him be at the same time. It's hard, no, almost impossible, to imagine a player of Lemieux's talent, potential, and expectation being afforded a similar opportunity to grow in such a fashion in places like New York, Chicago, or dare we wonder, the hockey hotbed of Montreal where the weight of the unworldly expectations would likely have been unbearable even for someone whose back proved to be as strong and resilient as Lemieux's. In

Pittsburgh the cheers were loud enough, the spotlight bright enough, but the space also large enough to make a perfect fit for his immensely private nature.

The scene at Pittsburgh's Point State Park, site of the Penguins' championship celebration days after returning home with the Stanley Cup, only solidified the relationship between Lemieux and the Pittsburgh fans. In his typically understated way, he offered the briefest yet deepest-resonating of speeches when it was his turn to address the massive crowd that turned out to celebrate the championship. He said a few kind words to the throngs of supporters then ended with a sincere and enthusiastic "this Cup's for you!" as everyone in attendance lost their collective minds over the sight of their icon hoisting the hardware for all to see.

Watching Pittsburgh and Lemieux mesh naturally over the years was a beautiful thing, neither asking too much of the other yet at the same time each expecting, and getting, so much along a two way street that had led them to NHL glory together. Lemieux had indeed become the most recognizable figure in Pittsburgh sports, and beyond that year's championship, with the surrounding cast in place it stood to reason that the Penguins' winning ways could continue for a long time to come.

Chapter 5 – Better than Everyone's Best…and Worst

It comes with the territory of being a superstar in any sport. Night in and night out, when you're the best you're going to get everyone else's best. With Lemieux clearly on top of his game entering the 1991-92 season, and the Penguins on top of the league, it meant only one thing – each opponent was going to go all out in an effort to knock Super Mario down a peg or two.

If you want to talk about points and power play goals and plus-minus and any other of the plethora of stat line figures that are part of measuring a hockey player's success, Lemieux mastered all of them in the 1991-92 campaign, just as he had for his entire career. What made the year so remarkable was that he did it all as the prime target night in and night out, the player around which each opponent's game plan was built, always including of an extra effort to stifle the game's top star.

He registered a hat trick just eleven days into the season in the Penguins' fifth game, a road tilt against the New York Islanders, after being held relatively in check in amassing only two goals and three assists through the first four contests. In an early December road drubbing of the expansion San Jose Sharks, an 8-0 Penguins' victory to be exact, Lemieux registered six points. On the day after Christmas he burned the Toronto Maple Leafs for seven points on two goals and five assists. Nights like those were simply Mario doing Mario things – putting up numbers that outpaced everyone else in the NHL. He led the league in points, finishing eight ahead of the next closest contender, not coincidentally his Pittsburgh teammate Kevin Stevens, despite playing in 16 fewer games.

But the individual marks took a back seat to Lemieux's leadership. His ability to make those around him better was evident in his teammates' success. Stevens not only recorded career highs in goals, assists, and points, he blew his previous season-best point total completely out of the water by more than 30. Larry Murphy enjoyed a career resurgence of sorts as he entered his 30's, falling just two goals short of his previous season-best total from five seasons prior. After a superb rookie campaign, Jagr was well on his way to becoming a full-fledged star in his own right, benefitting immeasurably from Lemieux's tutelage. Up and down the Penguins' roster Lemieux's impact on each and every player, and as a result on the caliber of the team, was clearly evident.

Despite starting the season looking every bit on pace to defend their Stanley Cup title, the Penguins' fortunes began to turn when 1992 arrived though. They won only three games in both January and February as injuries began to mount up. During those months, Lemieux missed stretches of four and six games, and by the first of March they were

Chapter 5 – Better than Everyone's Best…and Worst

only one game above the .500 mark and trying to avoid the undesirable fate of missing the playoffs as a defending champion. Similar to the previous season though, the front office made a blockbuster move as the trade deadline approached and, in nearly identical fashion, it seemed to energize and revitalize the Penguins. As part of a three-way deal with Los Angeles and Philadelphia, the Penguins sent Coffey to the Kings, Recchi to the Flyers, and received winger Rick Tocchet, defenseman Kjell Samuelsson, and goaltender Ken Wregget from Philadelphia.

Lemieux played at a torrid pace in March, notching 12 goals for his highest monthly total of the season and 24 points overall. Tocchet's scoring ability and toughness fit in nicely, and the Penguins surged to a 10-3-1 record, including a 7-0 mark at home, to climb back into the thick of the playoff race. Though they were too far behind to chase down the eventual Patrick Division champion Rangers, or even the Capitals for the second seed and home ice advantage, they were clearly peaking at the right time after their earlier lull.

The Penguins finished in third place and drew the Capitals as their opening round playoff opponent. From the beginning, the series proved to be dramatically different from the 4-1 victory the Penguins skated to with relative ease when the two teams met in the previous postseason. Lemieux was held out of Game 1 with a shoulder injury, and motivated by their home crowd, the Capitals won 3-1. Two nights later Lemieux was back in the lineup and assisted on two Pittsburgh goals, but the result was no different. Washington exploded on offense and after winning 6-2 was clearly in control as the series headed back to Pittsburgh.

If the previous year's championship run was any indication though, an early-series deficit was far from a precursor to the Penguins' undoing. True to form, they found their swagger again upon returning to the Civic Arena ice. Pittsburgh returned the favor to Washington in Game 3, notching their own offensive outburst that included a four goal second period. During that stretch Lemieux factored into every one of the Penguins' four scores, assisting on three and getting the puck past Washington goaltender Don Beaupre once himself. For the game he had a hat trick and three assists for a monstrous six-point night and more critically, a 6-4 Pittsburgh win that made it seem as if all was again well in the Penguins' world.

But as the adage goes, appearances can most definitely be deceiving. Despite the jolt of momentum from their scintillating Game 3 performance, the Penguins came out flat, uninspired, and about every other underwhelming adjective one could think of in Game 4. Lemieux scored a goal, one of the lone bright spots for Pittsburgh on what was an otherwise very forgettable night. The game wasn't just a Capitals' victory, it was a drubbing. The final tally was 7-2 Washington, and as a result the Penguins found themselves in dire

Chapter 5 – Better than Everyone's Best…and Worst

circumstances down 3-1 in the series as it shifted back to the nation's capital.

The Penguins began their uphill battle by speaking all of the right "one game at a time" adages that are commonplace in sports, but there was nothing common about the way they clawed back into the series. In a dramatic turn of fortune from the first two games in Washington, the Penguins thwarted the Capitals' offensive attack and found their own scoring power on the way to a 5-2 victory that sent the series back to Pittsburgh and gave them a glimmer of hope. That glimmer became a brilliant flame as the Penguins played inspired hockey in Game 6 to secure a 6-4 victory and give fans reason to believe they really could complete the unthinkable comeback two nights later in Washington.

Lemieux led the way with two goals and three assists for a team-high five points. His two goals, the Penguins' fifth and sixth of the game, came after the contest was knotted 4-4 as his resolve to not let his team's championship defense come to an end went on display for all to see. On the first, he stick-faked Beaupre multiple times from close range to get the Capitals' net minder sprawled on the ice and out of position before poking the puck home to give Pittsburgh the lead. Shortly after, he blistered a backhand from a sharp angle between the faceoff circles that was also no match for Beaupre and put the game securely in Pittsburgh's favor. In a show of emotion far greater than normal, Lemieux celebrated the goal by emphatically pumping his fist in celebration as if to show that the Penguins were entirely intent on knocking the Capitals out when they returned to Washington for the deciding game.

Lemieux got the Penguins off and running in Game 7 by scoring the team's first goal, and he followed by feeding Jagr for the next Pittsburgh score, which proved to be the game winner. Barrasso was brilliant in net, allowing only one Washington shot past him. When Joey Mullen rifled the puck into an empty Washington goal with under a minute left, the unthinkable comeback had become reality.

The Penguins had fended off elimination three consecutive times, had come back from a 7-2 home defeat in Game 4 that many thought left them with no wind remaining in their sails, and won two of three games on Washington ice to earn their way into the Patrick Division Finals against the Rangers. They received crucial contributions from every player up and down the roster that enabled them to do so, but clearly the one constant was Lemieux's focus and will to not be defeated. That will and resolve would face yet another challenge when the Penguins arrived at Madison Square Garden to begin the following series.

Despite not only winning the Patrick Division that year but also notching the best overall record in the NHL to claim the Presidents' Trophy, the Rangers faced their own seven-game battle in the opening series against New Jersey. New York

Chapter 5 – Better than Everyone's Best…and Worst

went down two games to one and also failed to close out the pesky Devils in Game 6 after retaking the series lead, but ultimately prevailed in Game 7 on home ice. The Penguins carried their momentum into the opener, and got goals from Troy Loney, Francis, Murphy, and Stevens along with two helpers from Lemieux to silence the New York crowd and claim the early series lead with a 4-2 victory.

But just when it seemed as if things were rolling right along for the Penguins, it happened. The "getting everyone's worst" part of the equation. It was confirmation of what Pittsburgh fans had already known well, that teams were absolutely inclined to try to bring down Lemieux in hopes that with him the Penguins' fortunes would correspondingly crumble. With the Penguins leading 1-0 in the first period of Game 2, New York's Adam Graves delivered a two-handed swing of his stick to Lemieux's left wrist in open ice that felled the Penguins' superstar and ultimately resulted in a fractured hand.

Every detail of the act gave the appearance of deliberateness, despite attempts from the Rangers' camp to deny it. Graves' swing looked like something that belonged in a different New York sporting venue several blocks north in the Bronx, and the fact that there wasn't a single player from either team within several feet of the event made any notion that it was a result of the pair just getting "tangled up" in the course of play seem largely impossible. It looked very much as if the Rangers had executed an intentional attack on Lemieux aimed at taking him out of the series, which ultimately came to be. To make matters even more infuriating for the Penguins, Graves was assessed only a two-minute penalty for the foul – hardly fair penance for an act that cost the Penguins the best player in the game.

Not only was Graves on the ice while Lemieux was out indefinitely as the series shifted to Pittsburgh two nights later, the newest public enemy in Pittsburgh also notched a goal in the Rangers' 6-5 overtime victory to retake home ice advantage. The loss ignited a fire within the Penguins though, and they reeled off three consecutive victories afterward including an inspiring overtime win in Game 4 and a victory at Madison Square Garden in Game 5 to shock the Rangers and win the series even without their superstar.

Lemieux's recovery progress was by far the primary topic of discussion throughout Pittsburgh during the four day break between the completion of the series and the opening game of the Wales Conference Finals. The Penguins' opponent for the conference crown was a familiar one. The Boston Bruins awaited, well-rested after a surprising four game sweep of the Montreal Canadiens and primed for revenge after the previous year's playoff outcome. Pittsburgh held home ice advantage despite finishing lower in their own division, third as opposed to the Bruins' second, by virtue of their higher regular season point total. If they were forced to play without

Chapter 5 – Better than Everyone's Best…and Worst

their top weapon though, it was hardly an understatement to say that home ice or not the Penguins would be at a severe disadvantage.

Fortunately they didn't have to find out what such a shorthanded state would be like. Although initial estimates pegged Lemieux to possibly be out for the remainder of the playoffs, he was suited up and back in the starting lineup for Game 2, a mere 14 days after taking the vicious slash from Graves. The Penguins squeezed out a dramatic 4-3 overtime victory in Game 1 as Jagr scored the game winner. To their credit, they played brilliantly throughout Lemieux's entire absence, but there was simply no denying that they were at their best with him back on the ice.

Lemieux made his presence felt immediately upon his return, torching the Bruins for two goals and an assist in a lopsided 5-2 victory that put Pittsburgh up 2-0 in the series as it shifted to Boston. In Game 3 Stevens stole the show in front of his hometown crowd. The Boston area native erupted for four goals and the Penguins again routed the Bruins, this time to the tune of 5-1. Lemieux didn't score but had three assists, and the Penguins sat a game away from a return trip to the Stanley Cup Finals.

The knockout blow came two nights later. Pittsburgh defeated Boston in Game 4 by the same 5-1 margin to complete the sweep. Lemieux, a bulky protective guard on his left wrist, led the way, scoring two goals. One was a brilliant display of speed and stickhandling as he took the puck in the neutral zone and blew by the Bruins' Bourque before beating Moog on a breakaway, dragging the puck between Bourque's legs not far from the very same spot on the ice where he had stolen it from him to initiate his first career goal.

An interesting matchup awaited in the finals. The Penguins were clearly firing on all cylinders after having battled back against Washington in the opening round, weathering the storm of Lemieux's injury in the division finals, and then parlaying his return into an utter dismantling of the Bruins in the conference championship. Their opponents, the Chicago Blackhawks, were playing equally well if not better. Chicago swept their opponents in both the division and conference finals, and hadn't lost since Game 3 of the opening round – a streak that was greater than a month long by the time the Stanley Cup Finals got underway in Pittsburgh.

It was then that Lemieux delivered yet another of his signature performances for the ages in Game 1. His bank shot off of Balfour's leg to bring Pittsburgh to within a goal after they had spotted Chicago a three-goal lead gave the Civic Arena crowd life. Not long after, his score in the game's final seconds to break the tie and give the Penguins the most unthinkable of victories gave the 16,000-plus fans in attendance and the droves watching on television or listening on the radio not just reason to believe their Penguins could

Chapter 5 – Better than Everyone's Best…and Worst

again raise hockey's ultimate prize, but a sense of assurance that they would.

The rest of the series, while certainly not a formality, was nothing short of a coronation for the Penguins and of course, the game's best player. Lemieux scored twice more in the Penguins' Game 2 victory, and when a Tom Barrasso shutout masterpiece in Game 3 at Chicago Stadium put them on the precipice of repeat glory, Lemieux capped off his second consecutive Conn Smythe winning performance with a goal and two assists as the Penguins defeated Chicago 6-5 in Game 4 to win the Stanley Cup for the second year in a row.

It was in the truest sense, a win for the ages. While the first to deflect praise to his teammates, nearly every single one of whom played brilliantly during the Penguins' repeat championship run, Lemieux had firmly etched his name among the list of all-time NHL greats. Through not just his brilliant play but, even more inspiringly, his ability to fight through injuries, to overcome clear and blatant attempts by opponents to physically hinder his contribution to Pittsburgh's attack well beyond the point of mere gamesmanship, and ultimately his ability to deliver in the most critical moments, Lemieux had overcome the best – and worst – that the NHL could throw at him during the 1991-92 season in leading the Penguins to another championship.

Chapter 6 – Hockey Was Only Half the Story

When sports and real life intersect it's next to impossible, despite all the opportunities for analogies or parallels or any other form of equating the two, to truly describe one in the context of the other. For in the end, there simply isn't any juxtaposing a game, even at its highest level and under its brightest lights, where the pressure and the demands and the stakes are so high, with anything that impacts one's very well being. That's not to say many a writer doesn't try, or even that it's wrong to do so. For part of the beauty of sports is that it offers an outlet, a window to try to understand far more serious matters. But a direct correlation? Impossible.

The 1992-93 Penguins began the season rolling right along in their quest to further solidify their legacy. Already back-to-back defending champions, the 1992-93 team was viewed by many as even better than either of the two previous championship clubs. Talk of a "three-peat" had steadily grown from mere fan boasting to a very possible end state given the way the Penguins blitzed through the first half of the season. Lemieux's play was, not at all surprisingly, a key factor in the Penguins' breakneck start. Through 40 games he amassed 39 goals and 104 total points, both astonishing numbers. He was on pace for just shy of a 220-point campaign, and surpassing Gretzky's NHL single season record of 215 points seemed a very real possibility.

Chapter 6 – Hockey Was Only Half the Story

Times were indeed good for the Penguins as they marched along the path seemingly paved for another championship run and guided by an even-better-than-anyone-thought-possible performance from Lemieux, at least for those who hadn't already learned that there was really no such thing since every game, every shift, brought with it the excitement and wonder of what other-worldly feat he'd pull off next.

And then it happened.

On January 12th, 1993 Lemieux, joined by his doctors and the Penguins' brass, held a press conference in front of reporters from across the United States and Canada to announce that he had been diagnosed with Hodgkin's disease, a form of cancer that affects the body's lymphatic system. The announcement cast a somber cloud over not only the Pittsburgh fans and the entire hockey world, but so much of the population in general given Lemieux's high-profile standing that made him recognizable beyond just sports circles. It was the kind of news that reiterated the sobering fact that despite anyone's prowess and irrespective of their current place in the prime of their career and more critically, of their very life, we're all so equally mortal. But after the initial devastation that Lemieux said brought him to tears during the entire trip home from the doctor's office upon learning his diagnosis, after the setback – again, it happened.

March 2nd…of the *same year*, to be exact. Just 49 days after the announcement that shocked and worried so many, there it was. A sporting rarity for sure, but an expression of human appreciation for all that an individual had gone through during those 49 days that was bigger than sports and divisional rivalries and different jerseys and all of that trivial stuff. A scene so polarizing that, while there really is no way to justifiably describe real life in the context of sports, came about as close as any possibly could in showing the magnitude of the situation.

Flyers fans – the very same ones that booed, and far worse, anybody wearing Pittsburgh black and gold out of sheer principle – gave Lemieux a standing ovation as he inexplicably returned to the Penguins' lineup for a Penguins road tilt in Philadelphia.

Lemieux scored a goal and added an assist that night, and while impressive given that he completed his final radiation treatment in Pittsburgh just hours earlier that morning, a physically draining regimen that can make simply going about normal daily activities difficult let alone hopping a plane and jumping right back into professional sports without missing a beat, it wasn't the real story. The Flyers ended up winning the game, if anyone remembers the actual outcome, and while it technically counted for two points in the Patrick Division standings, making it two points that the Penguins failed to capture, that quite frankly didn't matter one bit either.

Because the real story that night was the sheer remarkability of Lemieux's resolve in returning to the game at all, let alone so quickly. Of navigating his course of treatment with the same tenacity that he – here we go again with it being

Chapter 6 – Hockey Was Only Half the Story

impossible to intertwine life and sports and do the more significant one justice – showed when charging toward the goal on a breakaway, and the real winners that night were not only anyone fighting cancer but anyone facing any sort of difficult personal challenge from which they could draw inspiration from Lemieux's example. How many times over the decades since, and the years that will follow, for as long as Lemieux remains a prominent figure and even beyond that given the legacy he has established, has someone facing an uphill battle said "if Mario Lemieux did what he did then I can do this" to motivate themselves?

Probably way more than we'll ever know.

One thing that there's definitely way more of thanks to Lemieux's battle is support and resources for cancer patients and their families in the greater Pittsburgh area. In the time preceding the diagnosis, Lemieux was a notable figure in a variety of fundraising efforts and other charitable causes no different than so many other celebrities. Genuine, no doubt, but hardly akin to being a survivor oneself and using that most captivating of platforms to do good for others who face the same battle.

That year his determination on the ice became accompanied by another project for which he poured in the same passion and drive, the Mario Lemieux Foundation. Established to raise funds for cancer research and to support patients and their families, it has endured as a lasting symbol of hope forged upon Lemieux's successful battle and subsequent desire to use his standing and stature to help others. The figures are far more brilliant than any goal total or point record – tens of millions of dollars raised in the fight against cancer – and the scope of what it has built in Pittsburgh dwarfs a few hockey trophies any day.

Things like the Mario Lemieux Lymphoma Center at the University of Pittsburgh Medical Center (UPMC) Children's Hospital. The UPMC Lemieux Center for Patient Care and Research. The Lemieux Family Center, a place for families to find comfort and support throughout the transition between hospital and home care. The Mario Lemieux Center for Blood Cancers. The Austin's Playroom project, an idea Lemieux and his wife Nathalie came up with when their son Austin was born prematurely in 1996 and they noticed a lack of in-hospital options to engage their other two children, both toddlers. The list goes on and on.

And money has been the least of it.

The one place where Lemieux's private nature gets put on hold is in making appearances in support of his foundation. He's cut ribbons and given speeches and posed for photos galore and, more importantly, made visits and phone calls to so many patients, many of them children, to share his story and offer inspiration. At the Foundation's annual 6.6K race in 2016 he was on hand at the finish line to personally congratulate participants as they completed the course. He's donned a helmet, a bulletproof one, not the rounded Jofa that he made famous in his playing days, and a body armor vest to

Chapter 6 – Hockey Was Only Half the Story

dedicate Austin's Playrooms on military installations throughout the country.

It's all come about as a result of his harrowing experience in 1993, a superstar on the ice taking a difficult situation and using it to do super things for the city that supported him through the recovery process. And recover he did. It goes without saying that to merely resume any semblance of hockey-related activity that season would have been admirable of Lemieux, but his actions made it abundantly clear that his plans were always for much more.

The images are a lasting part of Pittsburgh sports history and speak volumes about the way Lemieux navigated his challenges. The turtleneck under his jersey to cover up the areas of his neck that were left tender from radiation treatments. The Sports Illustrated cover featuring Lemieux with the headline *"Miracle on Ice"* that nobody in the hockey world thought was the least bit of a slight to the 1980 United States Olympic team as it was every bit appropriate.

A week after the emotional comeback in Philadelphia he made his first game appearance back on the Civic Arena ice, to the welcome of Pittsburgh's impassioned fans. Lemieux remained a fixture in the Penguins' lineup for the remainder of the regular season and, to the sheer amazement of pretty much everyone, he erased a ten point deficit over the season's final month and a half to overtake Buffalo's Pat LaFontaine for the season scoring title despite playing in 24 fewer games. The typifying moment of that dramatic charge came at

Madison Square Garden on April 9th, where less than a year earlier the Rangers couldn't beat him by hacking away at his hands and on that night still couldn't beat him regardless of what other methods they tried.

Lemieux scored five goals, tying a career high, as the Penguins routed New York 10-4. The performance drew another standing ovation from a usually unfriendly to Pittsburgh road crowd that simply couldn't deny its appreciation for the feat that it was fortunate enough to witness. After Lemieux's fifth and final goal Lange declared in one of his signature celebrations, "If you missed this one, shame on you for six weeks!" Maybe 66 weeks would have been more appropriate given the circumstances. Honestly, we could all watch hockey for the next 66 years and not see anything close to what Mario Lemieux did that season.

The Penguins rode the wave of Lemieux's comeback, not just in inspiration but in the very figurative boost that having the best player in the game back in the lineup brought, to an NHL-record 17-game winning streak to close the season. In addition to claiming the Presidents' Trophy as the top regular season club, the Penguins finished with a franchise-record 119 points and by all accounts looked unbeatable as the quest for a three-peat entered into the postseason.

Pittsburgh breezed through the opening round, jumping out to a 3-0 series lead against the vastly overmatched New Jersey Devils and going on to win the series 4-1. Lemieux scored five goals and added four assists, and it was typical Penguins

Chapter 6 – Hockey Was Only Half the Story

hockey as they barreled full steam ahead into another matchup that many hockey experts thought would also be relatively easy.

But funny things happens in sports, as in life, as everyone around the penguins clearly came to realize that year.

Being at the top of the mountain doesn't guarantee immunity from getting knocked down. And the Penguins were reminded of that in the harshest of sporting ways when the Patrick Division Finals rolled around. Their opponents, the New York Islanders, pulled off a surprise first-round victory against Washington in six games that was the franchise's first playoff series win since 1987. Though the magic seemed destined to come to a screeching halt against the two-time defending champions, the Islanders had other ideas.

New York stole Game 1 in Pittsburgh and managed to earn a split in both of the opening two-game sets at each venue. When the Penguins won game 5 in Pittsburgh to go up 3-2 it again seemed that the series was in hand, but the gritty Islanders club scratched out a victory back on Long Island in Game 6 to force a deciding Game 7 at the Civic Arena. That game, as Penguins fans remember all too vividly, didn't go according to plan. The Penguins lost Kevin Stevens to a viscous facial injury in the first period after he fell unconscious in midair while completing a check and landed face-first on the ice, and ultimately lost the game when New York's David Volek scored in overtime to cap off the surprising upset.

In the instant it took Volek to one time a shot from just inside the faceoff dot to Barrasso's left, the Penguins' run of NHL supremacy was over. Humbling, without a doubt, and in the midst of the stunned Civic Arena silence that was interrupted only by the celebratory cheers coming from the New York bench as the Islanders players poured onto the ice, it was hard for anyone rooting for the Penguins to think of anything but that present moment and what was supposed to be but ultimately wouldn't.

The benefit of hindsight though has made it abundantly clear that while they lost a second round playoff series, the Penguins, and all of Pittsburgh, gained so much more that year, chiefly due to the poise and courage displayed by their captain. From any angle and through any lens, Lemieux's performance in the 1992-93 season was beyond remarkable. For in his battle against cancer, Lemieux achieved a victory that over time meant far, far more than claiming a third Stanley Cup ever would have. Returning to the ice the way he did, as if he never missed a beat, was astounding. But that was only the hockey side of things.

That season Lemieux not only served as an inspiration to so many, but gained a platform to be so much more significant and impactful to the city than just being a hockey superstar, even as unworldly of one as he was, would have ever afforded him the ability to be. The way he handled such a tremendous life challenge – not an athletic one though he faced more than his fair share of those during his career as well – paved the

Chapter 6 – Hockey Was Only Half the Story

way for him to embark on a role as a beacon of Pittsburgh resolve and pride for years to come, a role he has filled just as well as that of athletic superstar.

Chapter 7 – An Unimaginable Save

It hit like a ton of bricks, still every bit as hard to take even given the history of devastating announcements surrounding Lemieux that had regularly interrupted his stellar career. The date was April 6th, 1997. In the midst of another brilliant campaign that would ultimately lead to his fourth consecutive Ross Trophy, even with the Penguins remaining inside of the Eastern Conference playoff cut line throughout the season despite a number of ups and downs, Lemieux delivered news that sent shock waves throughout the hockey world. He was retiring from the NHL at the end of the season, whenever that would come for the Penguins.

There were several who had suspected in recent months that such a massive decision might be in the works given his increased irritation with the state of the game. His frustration, more toward the end of downright infuriation, with the NHL's reluctance to enforce interference rules was no secret by that point in his career. He spoke openly about how the holding and tackling that had become commonplace prevented skilled players like himself from being able to make plays at the level they were capable of. Add to that his physical challenges over the years, and it all seemed to make sense. Nonetheless though, actually hearing the official word from Lemieux himself shocked the legions of Penguins fans to say the least.

Chapter 7 – An Unimaginable Save

He was still in his prime as his play was clearly demonstrating, despite all of the aforementioned physical ailments. In his prime, at least, meaning he was better than everyone else in the league, even if he wasn't reaching his absolute optimal level of performance. Pittsburgh fans hoped there were at least a few more years left to enjoy and appreciate Lemieux's play, but instead were suddenly faced with the reality that they had four more regular season games and whatever the Penguins could manage in the playoffs left to watch their superstar before he skated off into the sunset.

The news had a devastating impact on morale among the Pittsburgh fan base. Local radio station WDVE put together a parody version of the Don McLean song *American Pie* that captured how pretty much everyone in the city felt upon hearing it, with one verse stating:

> *Well we know his back is pretty sore*
> *And he's not a young guy anymore*
> *But when he kicks off the skates*
> *He leave us second rate*
> *We were knockin' on the basement floor*
> *When we drafted him in '84*
> *How in the world can we endure?*
> *The day Lemieux retired*

The Penguins limped into the playoffs losing three of their remaining four games after Lemieux's announcement. The sixth seed in the Eastern Conference, they opened the postseason in Philadelphia and lost the first two games of the series, further hammering home the reality for Pittsburgh fans that the upcoming two contests at the Civic Arena were likely to be their last opportunity to see Lemieux play. After a Game 3 loss put the Penguins on the brink of elimination and Lemieux's career on the verge of its final act, he delivered one more magical Mario moment in the closing moments of Game 4.

With Pittsburgh ahead 3-1, avoiding a sweep and fighting to stay alive for at least one more game, Lemieux was on the ice with just over a minute remaining and it was no secret to anyone what he, and the Penguins, were trying to cook up. But secret or not, the way it unfolded was, in a word, magical. Winger Ian Moran was able to steal the puck in the Penguins' zone, and without looking simply backhanded it up the side boards, almost instinctively knowing who would be there to receive it. As soon as it touched Lemieux's stick near the red line, he was off to the races one final time as the Civic Arena crowd gasped in collective anticipation.

There was, of course, no other possible ending.

Lemieux buried the puck past Flyers' goalie Garth Snow, and the crowd erupted louder than any crowd cheering for a team that was down 3-1 in a playoff series ever had. One more time for the fans that had rode the highs of two Stanley Cups and the lows of his health troubles with him to bask in the

Chapter 7 – An Unimaginable Save

aftermath of a breakaway goal. One more time to hear Civic Arena public address announcer John Barbero's signature call that a Pittsburgh goal had been scored by "number sixty-six, Mario Lemieuuuuuuuuuuuuuuuux."

It was, to the extent possible at least, some degree of closure for Penguins fans. The post-goal cheers went on for several minutes, much longer than they normally did. A few hats came onto the ice despite the goal being Lemieux's only one of the game, emblematic of the dozens of times he had scored three or even more goals and caused so many fans to gladly part with their headgear in celebration. He received a standing ovation and made a brief acknowledgement by raising his stick, but then it was done. The Penguins not surprisingly lost the following game in Philadelphia two days later despite Lemieux recording a goal and an assist, and just like that, the Mario Lemieux era in Pittsburgh was over.

Or so it seemed.

The Hockey Hall of Fame waived the required three-year waiting period and inducted Lemieux that fall, indicative of the impact he had on the game. But when the following NHL season got underway, the "new" version of Penguins hockey that was on display in Pittsburgh was in many ways unremarkable for a fan base trying to find its way post-Lemieux. Everything felt different, even though the club still featured a number of star players that were popular with the fans, namely Jagr. The Penguins made the playoffs in 1998 after their first season playing without Lemieux, but were summarily bounced in the opening round by Montreal. Of far greater interest in Pittsburgh though was what happened a few weeks after the season came to a close.

Despite signing a guaranteed seven-year, $42 million contract in 1992, Lemieux had yet to receive a large portion of the money due to him. In simple terms, the bill for the championship clubs the Penguins' leadership had assembled through their numerous high-profile trades and free agent signings in the early 1990's had finally come due. Through the middle portion of the decade the team asked multiple times, and Lemieux agreed, to defer some of his salary payments in order to help ease its struggling financial situation.

In 1997 the Penguins' ownership group of Howard Baldwin, Morris Belzberg, and Thomas Ruta brought on retired tech mogul Roger Marino as a fourth partner to provide financial support. The situation quickly deteriorated however, as the parties failed to get along. Baldwin and Marino ultimately ended up in a feud, each seeking to buy the other's share in order to become majority owner.

After multiple iterations of trying to collect the money owed to him and a firm belief that Marino was seeking any way possible for the Penguins to back out of his contract, Lemieux sued Marino and the Penguins in June of 1998 for nearly $33 million in back salary payments. The Penguins were ultimately

Chapter 7 – An Unimaginable Save

forced to file for Chapter 11 bankruptcy as the franchise had gone nearly $100 million in debt. The entire situation, messy and bleak as it looked, was actually the perfect storm. Among the droves of individuals and businesses that the Penguins owed money to, their largest creditor was, of course, Lemieux.

And so began a storyline so unimaginable that the only way it could come to be is if it involved Lemieux. It had a classic "knight in shining armor rides in on a gallant horse to save the day" aura to it. Lemieux, instead of simply seeing the legal process through to collect from the Penguins, formulated a plan for the team's debt to him to instead be converted into equity, making him the majority owner. It was unprecedented in major professional sports, but then again, so much of what Lemieux had done throughout his brilliant career was defined by that term that it almost made perfect sense.

What would absolutely need to make perfect sense though, were the hard details of the plan. For as great as the idea was, the reality of the situation was that Lemieux wasn't a big time businessman, and the Penguins were mired deep in a financial mess that featured multiple layers of complexity. To get past the "rah-rah" good sentiment that it conjured up and actually make his vision viable required an inordinate amount of work, and more selling than any of Lemieux's beautiful breakaway moves that faked many a goaltender into the first row of seats ever did.

The first hurdle of course was convincing both the court and the NHL that ownership by Lemieux and the small group of his close confidants that he'd assembled to help him work through the process was the best course of action for the struggling Penguins. Critical to that was showing that in addition to Lemieux's equity stake, as well as a contribution of his own money he opted to put up, he had had the necessary operating cash to make his plan workable. Securing investors became the first order of business, and as his team prepared to present their plan to NHL Commissioner Garry Bettman in the spring of 1999 Lemieux's attorney Chuck Greenburg indicated that the group had indeed secured a viable large investor.

That person, of course, turned out to be billionaire Ron Burkle, a California native who made a substantial fortune in the supermarket and technology industries and with an investment portfolio that spanned multiple companies. To this day there are plenty in Pittsburgh that still wouldn't recognize him if he sat down right in front of them, and judging from his propensity to keep a low profile, Burkle would have things no other way. Matched through mutual connections, Lemieux and Burkle combined to form exactly what the Penguins needed – healthy financial support from an investor who was willing to step out of the way and let the hockey superstar and Pittsburgh hero be the face of the franchise.

Chapter 7 – An Unimaginable Save

Adding Burkle gave Lemieux's group the hard credibility that it needed, beyond the simple goodwill that Pittsburgh felt toward him. The group gained approval of the bankruptcy court, and on September 1st, 1999 the NHL's Board of Governors approved Lemieux's application for ownership. To say it was a monumental day in Pittsburgh would have been about as much of an understatement as saying Lemieux was a pretty good player. It was as if the cloudy skies that had plagued the Penguins since Lemieux hung up his skates two years prior finally opened up and let a golden ray of sunlight shine on the franchise again. The Penguins, by all accounts, were saved – by the only person who could have possibly done so.

Anyone else, even the most Pittsburgh of Pittsburghers, wouldn't have carried the clout that Lemieux did in stepping up to salvage what so many would have sadly written off as a sinking ship. Putting his name behind the Penguins, taking on a personal financial risk, made the climb out of distress seem not only possible for Penguins fans, it made it inspiring – another unimaginable Lemieux comeback. It made things feel right again, in a way that of course was different from his playing days yet comforting just the same.

It gave Pittsburgh fans the satisfaction of knowing that their beloved Penguins were finally in good hands again, Mario's hands. It elevated the feelings for Lemieux around Pittsburgh beyond what anyone could have ever thought possible because even though he clearly dealt in pay figures that were way out of the everyday person's league, he did something few, if any, everyday people would ever have the fortitude to do in going to bat to save an organization after it made multiple attempts to shortchange him in a mutual salary agreement.

Lemieux gave the Penguins a renewed future when quite frankly they had none. He brought them back from the brink of extinction, and he did it with the same tenacity that he exhibited as a player in guiding them to a championship level in the first place. When his group finally took ownership in the fall of 1999, the stories abounded of his directive that all of the Penguins' debts be paid back on the dollar, nearly unheard of in bankruptcy proceedings but a move that absolutely struck a chord with the local fan base that had become disenchanted by the team's previous financial mismanagement.

On October 7th, the Penguins played their first home game of the 1999-00 season at the newly-renamed Mellon Arena. Along with ownership of the team came the naming rights to the Civic Arena, which Lemieux's group sold to the financial services company, a mainstay in Pittsburgh for years. The Penguins were victorious, 7-5, over the Devils, giving things an almost classic feel. Fans enamored by the fact that Mario Lemieux would now be gracing the owner's box high above the ice harkened back to the days when Lemieux the player

Chapter 7 – An Unimaginable Save

led so many Pittsburgh comeback efforts, like the one the 1991 Stanley Cup championship club orchestrated against that same New Jersey franchise. In their minds, Lemieux had done it all. He had led the Penguins to greatness, then brought them back to life when they faced an almost certain demise.

But as they would soon come to find out, he was far, far from finished.

Chapter 8 – Back to the Future

One can only wonder how Jay Caufield did it.

How he kept what he knew to himself despite being privy to the juiciest news in all of Pittsburgh.

Actually, in all of sports.

After all, there is knowing things, and then there is *knowing* things – and Caufield's knowledge absolutely fell into the latter category. For several weeks in the fall of 2000 Caufield and Lemieux, teammates on the Penguins' Stanley Cup winning squads of the early 1990's that had remained close friends after each of their playing careers ended, met in the dark, pre-dawn hours. Their rendezvous spot was the Island Sports Complex, an open-to-the-public rink at Pittsburgh's Robert Morris University that was located just a short jaunt down the Ohio River from the big rink in town than Lemieux had helped adorn with the two Stanley Cup banners that hung from its rafters.

The secret meetings began when Lemieux, at the point of his retirement where the standard variety alumni and charity games were usually the most serious ice time a former player saw, made a call to Caufield asking if he were free to work out over the coming weeks. Caufield obliged, not knowing Lemieux's intentions at first but quickly finding out exactly

Chapter 8 – Back to the Future

what he had on his mind. It clearly wasn't playing in any alumni games.

Lemieux enlisted Caufield as his trainer and confidant to help him prepare to do what he swore he'd never do when he hung up the skates in 1997. What he insisted wasn't in the cards when he went through the process of assuming ownership of the Penguins the year prior. His health issues, his frustration with certain aspects of the game that had contributed to his decision to retire in the first place, his now full-time day job of owning the franchise – all were strong reasons to believe that Mario Lemieux coming back to play for the Penguins again would simply never happen. But after all, Lemieux's entire playing career as well as his handling of the Penguins' ownership situation had taught everyone one very important thing about him. Never say never.

So for Caufield, along with the rink manager who was also entrusted with the secret, both men knowing what was afoot even before Lemieux's own family did, the modus operandi was to not say a word. Caufield was a physical specimen who had similarly helped other teammates with their conditioning, and he put Lemieux through his paces as he attempted to work himself back into game shape. The vision and ability to see the game three steps ahead of anyone else was still there. The quick hands were still there. And after several grueling sessions with Caufield, the legs were beginning to get there as well. All of it led to an early-December announcement that, in typical Lemieux fashion, astounded and amazed everyone to the point of having to stop and consider if it were actually true.

He was indeed coming back.

It would be an unprecedented occurrence in major professional sports. The days of player-coaches were long gone, and no club had ever seen a player-owner. Naturally, there were questions. One of the most obvious was if he were doing it simply to sell tickets, equivalent to a publicity stunt. The world got its answer when during a press conference announcing his plans he fielded that exact question sternly, almost as if offended by it. He very directly stated that not only would an extra million dollars or so not make that significant of an impact for the Penguins' bottom line, indicating the work the organization had done to improve its financial health since his group had taken ownership, it wouldn't impact his personal way of life either. Translation: it wasn't any kind of stunt; it was for real.

He spoke of how changes in the way the game was officiated since his retirement were for the better, of play being more open and less restrictive for the finesse players as had so strongly frustrated him years earlier. He spoke of wanting his son Austin, born just before his retirement, to be able to have memories of seeing him play. And most telling, he spoke of the time away from the sport causing him to miss the opportunity to compete.

Chapter 8 – Back to the Future

Soon after, Lemieux and the Penguins set December 27th, a home game against the Toronto Maple Leafs, as his official comeback date. For that night Pittsburgh became the epicenter of the sports media world, in similar fashion to when Michael Jordan, a friend of Lemieux's who he mentioned having sought advice from on orchestrating a comeback, made his return to the NBA after a similar initial retirement. Television stations from across the United States and Canada clamored to deliver the story, and it turned out to be one that even the most imaginative of screenwriters couldn't possibly have cooked up.

After the opening fanfare had subsided, just 33 seconds into the game with the puck jammed deep in the Toronto zone, Lemieux dug it out from near the goal, centering it perfectly for Jagr to poke home, giving the Penguins a 1-0 lead. Visions of that night in Boston some 16 years prior when he scored on his first-ever shift raced through the minds of the capacity crowd as they reveled in hearing his name called as part of a Pittsburgh goal announcement again. But that was simply the warm up.

With the Penguins leading 2-0 midway through the second period, he took a pass from Jagr perfectly in stride while streaking down the center of the ice and buried a shot past Toronto goaltender Curtis Joseph. The goal sent the home crowd into the sort of bedlam they hadn't experienced since the Penguins' championship runs of nearly a decade prior. He added another assist for good measure before the 5-0 Penguins' victory was complete, marking a magical return to the ice.

Lemieux continued his strong play for the remainder of his comeback season, notching 76 points in only 43 games, the highest points per game average of any player in the league. He was named the Captain of the North American squad for the 2001 All Star game, tallying a goal and an assist in the midseason showcase. The Penguins as a team enjoyed success in parallel with Lemieux's comeback. They advanced to the Eastern Conference Finals, upsetting the Capitals in the opening round and then winning a seven game series against the Buffalo in the second, but ultimately fell to New Jersey in their bid to reach the Stanley Cup Finals.

That season, however, marked the end of the Penguins' run of playoff successes for several years to come. Still in the process of righting their financial ship, the Penguins were forced to part ways with Jagr during the offseason, dealing him to the Capitals. Lemieux also encountered a hip injury during the 2001-02 campaign that caused him to miss nearly three quarters of the team's schedule, and the Penguins fell to last place in the Atlantic Division, out of the playoffs. Lemieux rebounded for a mostly-healthy 2002-03 campaign and tallied 91 points, good for eighth in the league, but again the Penguins finished last in their division and failed to qualify for the postseason.

Chapter 8 – Back to the Future

After an injury-riddled 2003-04 campaign that saw Lemieux suit up for only 10 games, and the complete loss of the 2004-05 season due to the NHL lockout, he returned for the 2005-06 season. For Penguins fans it was a chance to see two generations of Pittsburgh superstars take the ice together, as the previous summer the Penguins secured highly-touted phenom Sidney Crosby with the top pick in the 2005 NHL draft in almost identical fashion to their drafting of Lemieux.

Selecting Crosby came with much of the same fanfare that had accompanied the Penguins' selection of Lemieux in 1984, visions of the youngster as team's heir apparent crossing many a mind. More than just an owner in the financial sense and more than just a team captain in the dressing room and on the ice, Lemieux opened his home to the teenager Crosby to offer a support system as he made the transition from junior hockey to the rigors of the NHL both on and off the ice.

Crosby's evolution into the next generation team leader in Pittsburgh, which happened alongside similar developmental paths for goaltender Marc-Andre Fleury and forward Evgeni Malkin, the Penguins' top draft picks each the two years prior, represented an ushering in of a new era of Penguins hockey. While the team still struggled through the early part of the 2000's, the future was immensely bright after its string of losing seasons enabled it to secure such a core nucleus of young talent. Lemieux, now the elder statesman of the club, continued playing and brought an immeasurable level of experience to the young Penguins.

That tutelage came to an abrupt end though in December of 2005 when Lemieux was hospitalized with an irregular heartbeat. Reports indicated he had been experiencing the condition in the weeks prior after becoming excessively winded while playing. After a series of tests he was diagnosed with atrial fibrillation, a condition that causes an irregular and at times rapid heart rate. While the positive was that the condition was wholly manageable, many saw the writing on the wall as it related to Lemieux's hockey career.

On January 24th, 2006 Lemieux announced he was retiring again. Citing the health issues he had encountered in his second stint as a player as well as his simple inability at 40 years of age to keep pace with the younger generation of players, he recognized it was finally time for him to end his playing days for good. The news was hardly a shock, in contrast to his first retirement announcement nearly a decade earlier. While the entire hockey community was saddened by the news, this exit had a natural sense to it, a feeling of happening at the right time rather than Lemieux trying to hang on longer than he should have.

In the months that followed though, after having fought through so many injuries and setbacks in both stages of his playing career, Lemieux faced another fight. It was waged in settings drastically different from doctors' offices or arenas,

Chapter 8 – Back to the Future

but Lemieux poured his all into is just as he had in battling the health aliments that so unfortunately had interrupted his brilliant career. Mellon Arena, home to so much history thanks largely in part to Lemieux himself during the days it operated under its original name, lagged greatly behind the rest of the venues in the NHL. At over 40 years old, it was the most dated building in the league, and in an era where the sports business model relied heavily on revenue from luxury suites and premium concession arrangements, the Igloo, as it had become known for its outer circular dome, was clearly a limiting factor in the Penguins' ability to be a financially viable franchise into the 2000's and beyond.

While Lemieux's successful bid to take ownership had kept the Penguins safe in Pittsburgh for the near term, getting a new arena was the only way to make keeping them in Pittsburgh for the long term possible. But, as Pittsburgh learned in having gone through the process of constructing new stadiums for both the Steelers and Pirates just a few years prior, how such a venture would be paid for was clearly the multi-million dollar question that no party to the discussion would volunteer to be the sole answer to.

In the years since he took over the Penguins, much of it going on simultaneously as he was training for his comeback, playing, mentoring the Penguins' young stars, and dealing with his own new health matters, Lemieux was also involved in a complex game of tug-of-war with local officials over the arena issue. Politicians held that any new venue should be funded with private money, while the Penguins sought a joint effort that would work out for everyone's benefit by keeping the team, and the associated economic stimulus it brought, in town.

There were reported promises, followed by reports of those same promises being broken. There were state and local election cycles that factored into the equation, legislators weighing their own political agendas against the demands of the man who could likely run for any office in western Pennsylvania and emerge victorious. There was the insertion of the NHL as is often the case with leagues when a team is mired in financial struggles, and the unwavering statement from NHL Commissioner Bettman that the Penguins simply couldn't survive in Pittsburgh absent a new facility. There was banter over casino money funding the new building that was predicated on the gaming company the Penguins had an agreement with being awarded one of the new licenses that the local government had voted to issue, then a subsequent curveball in the awarding of that license to another firm that forced Lemieux and the Penguins to scramble for an alternative plan.

There was Kansas City.

Perhaps more than any other element of the years-long negotiation process that Lemieux and the Penguins were involved in with the city, the rise of another suitor eager to

Chapter 8 – Back to the Future

sweep the Penguins away from Pittsburgh became the lynchpin to finally striking a deal. The home of the Royals and Chiefs rolled out the red carpet for Lemieux, offering a state of the art new facility rent free plus multiple other financial benefits if the team were to relocate. Kansas City businesses expressed their willingness to support bringing the team to town, and with no further ground being given at home it seemed like a very viable proposition that the Kansas City Penguins would come to be. Lemieux, who openly expressed his displeasure in feeling slighted by how the negotiation process up to that point played out with Pittsburgh, was left with no other option than to make one final figurative stick fake as the situation neared a point of reckoning.

With the Penguins' Mellon Arena lease set to expire, Lemieux announced that without a new building, the team would indeed seek to relocate. He and Burkle visited Kansas City, did all of the "shake and grin" maneuvers that would come with a budding new partnership, and sold it as well as anyone could. Retrospect shows, and his own recollection after the fact confirms, that Lemieux was in fact bluffing. But it was a bluff just as believable as the ones with which he crossed up many a hapless defender or faked out a multitude of goaltenders during his career. While Kansas City did indeed offer every single reason for Lemieux to move the Penguins during a time when, quite frankly, Pittsburgh wasn't offering nearly as many to stay, it was nothing more than posturing.

Brilliant posturing, that is.

Using the now-legitimized threat of leaving town as leverage, Lemieux and his group finally reached an agreement with state and local politicians on an arena deal. On March 13th, 2007 the two sides announced a plan that would effectively keep the Penguins in Pittsburgh for the next 30 years, and move them into a new arena in the coming years. All of the negotiations, all of the hardball, all of the finding another way and a Plan B and regrouping after one seemingly promising course of action after another fell through culminated in a gigantic victory for all of Pittsburgh.

It led to Lemieux being able to walk on to the Mellon Arena ice with a microphone that night and in less than a minute give the fans the best news they had heard since his name was called as the team's selection in the 1984 draft. In his typically understated way, he delivered a message that impacted the Pittsburgh fan base, especially those who had been along for the two plus decades since the relationship between Lemieux and Pittsburgh had started, to its core.

Their Pittsburgh Penguins, as he made it a point to emphasize to the fans, were staying put.

Chapter 9 – "See You at Center Ice"

With the arena matter solved it was as if the Penguins became free to blossom into everything they were meant to be in the post-Lemieux-as-a-player generation. They won in a shootout the night of his announcement and proceeded to have their best month of the 2006-07 season in March, finishing the month undefeated at home and surpassing the 100 point mark in the standings for the first time in over a decade. Their final tally of 105 points was nearly double that of the season prior, and clearly the lean years that led to the series of high draft picks were beginning to pay dividends as the team's young stars became prominent names among the NHL's top players.

They qualified for the playoffs as the fifth seed in the Eastern Conference, and though they were defeated in the opening round by the Ottawa Senators four games to one, it was clear to all involved that the new Penguins had arrived, and hopes for the future were high. How high those hopes would rise in such a short time though couldn't have been imagined by anyone. Unless, of course, they were viewing the situation through the lens of a club formed under the watchful eye of a presence like Lemieux's.

The following season the Penguins sold out every home game on the schedule for the first time in franchise history, a far cry from the state of affairs in the early part of the decade but strikingly similar in form to how the very same seats went from empty to full again after Lemieux's arrival as a player. While fans flocked through the turnstiles to see the likes of Crosby, Malkin, Fleury, and Jordan Staal, it clearly wasn't lost on anyone that it was all built upon one Pittsburgh legend's unwavering commitment to what the team could become and should remain.

The Penguins finished the season as Atlantic Division champions that year and entered playoffs as the second seed in the Eastern Conference. They again drew Ottawa as their first round opponent, and in a testament to how much the team had advanced, this time they swept the Senators in four games. They followed that series by nearly doing the same to the both the Rangers in the conference quarterfinals and the cross-state rival Flyers in the Eastern finals. In both series a Game 4 loss was the lone blemish on their card.

Game 5 against Philadelphia carried the kind of special, everything-has-come-full-circle feel to it that only a handful of games throughout a career or a lifetime as a fan can evoke. For all the team had been through in recent years, to again stand on the verge of competing for the Stanley Cup was a moving circumstance, to say the least. Even more moving was the way in which the Penguins rose to the occasion. The game was over, quite literally, just minutes after it started. Pittsburgh native Ryan Malone scored less than three minutes into the first period, and though the Penguins added five more

Chapter 9 – "See You at Center Ice"

goals for good measure, Malone's tally was all they'd need as Fleury pitched a shutout. As the final seconds ticked away, visions of the same scene against Boston in 1991 raced through the minds of so many who had steadfastly stood by their Penguins over the years.

Same building. Many of the same fans. Same floor-rattling, wall-shaking energy reverberating throughout, driven by the excitement of a team that was the league's worst in the not so distant past but now had the opportunity to become the best. And while the players on the ice were different, the one constant through it all was of course the man who had led the team during that first run of glory, then salvaged and rebuilt it, this time in a suit and tie instead of a jersey and skates, for the latest. The Penguins didn't win the Stanley Cup that year, falling to the Detroit Red Wings despite a frantic last ditch effort in the final seconds of Game 6 in front of that very same Mellon Arena crowd, but in terms of the evolution and rebirth of the franchise, they had indeed won so much.

The enthusiasm over the Penguins' dramatic run carried into the 2008 offseason and was complimented perfectly by a moment that so many thought would never become a reality. On a sunny August afternoon, wearing construction hardhats with Penguins logos affixed to the sides, Lemieux joined then-Pennsylvania Governor Ed Rendell and then-Pittsburgh Mayor Luke Ravenstahl alongside several members of the Penguins' front office for a groundbreaking ceremony at the site of what would become center ice for the team's new arena.

The ceremony, complete with all of the photos, hand-shaking, and everything else common to such events, represented the coming to fruition of Lemieux's vision of the Penguins as a permanent part of Pittsburgh. While just a patch of dirt, one couldn't help but wonder about the moments that would take place at that very site when the arena was complete, the ice freshly surfaced and the red center line drawn, for the current generation of Penguins as well as squads well into the franchise's future.

Shortly after the groundbreaking, the 2008-09 campaign opened with high hopes for the Penguins to again contend for the Stanley Cup. Midway through the season though they were merely treading water, barely above .500 and on the outside of the Eastern Conference playoff race looking in. The subpar performance compared to expectations was the primary driver behind a February coaching change that saw Michel Therrien ousted and replaced by Dan Bylsma, who at the time was behind the bench of the Penguins' AHL affiliate in Wilkes-Barre/Scranton. The Penguins executed a remarkable late-season turnaround under Bylsma, finishing 18-3-4 down the stretch and earning the fourth seed in the Eastern Conference playoffs.

The Penguins' postseason run then set the stage for yet another defining Lemieux moment that will remain forever in

Chapter 9 – "See You at Center Ice"

the minds of many a Pittsburgh fan and hockey historian. Riding their late-season momentum, the Penguins defeated the Flyers, Capitals, and Carolina Hurricanes in succession to again reach the Stanley Cup Finals. Just as in the year prior, their opponent was the Red Wings. The series opened in Detroit where the home squad won both of the first two games to seize a commanding lead as the series shifted to Pittsburgh.

Home ice, and clearly the Pittsburgh home crowd, proved to be exactly what the Penguins needed to climb back into the series however. They notched victories in both Game 3 and Game 4 to even the slate heading back to Detroit. Game 5 though didn't go at all as hoped for. Detroit blasted the Penguins 5-0 to move to within one victory of repeating as champions. The disheartening defeat combined with the uphill battle of having to beat the Red Wings in back to back games, including a potential Game 7 in Detroit, seemed insurmountable. There was the standard talk of how the Penguins' stars were still young with plenty of good years and championship runs ahead of them. Of how the Red Wings were simply a juggernaut that couldn't be beaten. And of how just making the Finals in back to back years was an amazing feat for any team, let alone given where the franchise was just a few years prior.

But to any true Penguins fan, none of it was anything worth hearing. Pittsburgh was a proud sports town, and losing in a championship final wasn't something that happened often for any of its teams. The thought of it occurring to the Penguins in back to back seasons left a bitter taste in the mouths of many – including the Penguins players themselves, it would turn out. Pittsburgh won an inspiring Game 6 at home 2-1, the contest forever remembered for Lange's famous "I'll meet ya in the schoolyard baby for all the marbles, Friday night in Detroit" call.

But before Friday night, before the two teams took to the Joe Louis Arena ice for one final game to settle the score and determine which one would skate around one of hockey's most venerable buildings with its highest prize, something else happened. As the story goes, Lemieux was back in Pittsburgh Thursday evening, exchanging text messages with several members of the team's front office and coaching staff in Detroit before he departed on his way to join them. Never the rah-rah type, and especially not in his role as owner, he shocked the entire contingent when he sent a short yet powerful message that he asked be delivered to each the players' phones so they would awake to it game day morning:

"This is a chance of a lifetime to realize your childhood dream to win a Stanley Cup. Play without fear and you will be successful! See you at center ice."

See you at center ice.

From the man who hundreds of times throughout his career left lasting images of the black and gold Penguins sweater

Chapter 9 – "See You at Center Ice"

streaking down the center of the ice on the way to another breakaway goal, who twice wore the skating Penguin crest at center ice while as team captain being the first to raise the Stanley Cup, who just months earlier had broken ground at the site of what was to be the team's *new* center ice, securing its future when so many had written it off as on its way out of town; from the face of Penguins hockey and one of, if not the most prominent sports star in a city with as great a lineage of sports stars as any, they were five powerful words that propelled the Penguins to a most improbable victory.

Pittsburgh defeated the Red Wings in that Game 7, fending off a final-second barrage of Detroit shots to maintain a 2-1 advantage. They became the first NHL team in 38 years to win Game 7 of the Stanley Cup Finals on the road and the first team in any of the four major professional sports in 30 years, the previous one being another proud part of Pittsburgh's championship heritage, the 1979 Pirates, to win Game 7 of a championship series away from home. After the bedlam that ensued in front of the Penguins' goal had subsided, Lemieux's words rang true.

See you at center ice.

17 years after having last lifted the Stanley Cup as a player, Mario Lemieux became the only person to have their name inscribed on it as a team owner as well. The Penguins returned home to a crowd of nearly 400,000 who turned out along Pittsburgh's Grant Street and Boulevard of the Allies a few

days later to salute their Penguins. Lemieux, joined by Burkle, took a back seat to the players as they paraded the hardware in front of the impassioned fans, but his presence, and impact in making all of what had come about for the Penguins, was clearly evident to all.

A year and a few short months later, the Penguins hosted the Flyers in the opener to the 2010-11 NHL season. It had all of the expected pomp and circumstance of an opening night game, but it also had something extra. It was, of course, the first regular season game played in the Penguins' new home, the Consol Energy Center. A brilliant, state-of-the-art venue that boasted all of the niceties and amenities that made it one of the premier buildings in the league but more importantly, the key to making the Penguins the *Pittsburgh* Penguins for decades to come. Before the game got underway, there was a ceremony to acknowledge the moment, highlighted in the only way possible.

See you at center ice.

Those fabled motivating words prior to Game 7 of the Stanley Cup Finals sixteen months earlier were just as fitting for the evening at hand. Lemieux, in a suit but with hockey skates on, came to center ice and from his jacket pocket revealed a crystal decanter containing water that was from the melted ice of the Penguins' former home. He poured it onto the new surface to represent a merging of generations, a link for the

Chapter 9 – "See You at Center Ice"

Penguins' present day successes to the franchise's championship history of the past.

The years that followed brought tremendous regular season accomplishments for the Penguins, but of course, as everyone knows, there was one glaring omission. For each impressive result through the first 82 games there was an equally unimpressive postseason, culminating in a premature exit that, in a town that values its championships as much as Pittsburgh, didn't quite sit well. Realizing that the team was in the thick of the best years for its stars, who after time had started creeping up on them no longer had the adjective "young" placed in front of them by default, many around Pittsburgh wondered if the Penguins' second dynasty that seemed so inevitable when they skated to the Finals two years in a row would never come to be.

Along the way though, something else happened. Something that showed the true feelings of Pittsburghers toward Lemieux and spoke volumes about his impact on the city, and the fans' appreciation of all he had done. In June of 2015 reports surfaced, which the Penguins quickly confirmed, that Lemieux and Burkle had engaged a consulting firm to help them explore options for a possible sale of the franchise. That wasn't surprising – after all, they'd owned the team together for going on 16 years, guided it out of bankruptcy to the point where it was ranked by Forbes as one of the most valuable professional sports franchises in the world, and of course was on solid footing in Pittsburgh for years to come. With the appreciation in value that accompanied all of those accomplishments, it seemed only logical that any businessperson might deem it a good time to realize a return on their investment.

What was remarkable was that so much of the sentiment toward the potential situation was one of happiness for Lemieux. Fans spoke of being sad to see the Penguins leave his control if he were to sell, but moreover of how he, more than anyone, deserved every penny of the windfall payday he'd receive. No mention of feeling slighted, of feeling as if they were being left. No talk of backing out on the team because clearly, undeniably, Lemieux had gone above and beyond multiple times over the course of his multiple decades in Pittsburgh to put the Penguins, and as a result the fans, first and foremost. They understood, and they recognized the opportunity Lemieux had in front of him and in an odd yet also understandable way, many wanted it for him.

But, for a variety of reasons, most of which we'll never know, it didn't happen. There were reports that Lemieux and Burkle weren't aligned on the asking price, some going as far as to say the pair had an offer on the table that Lemieux was willing to accept but that Burkle wasn't. Quickly and professionally, they issued a statement to the contrary, simply saying that they were continuing to review all options. That continued review of options just happened to lead into the 2016 NHL playoffs.

Chapter 9 – "See You at Center Ice"

In a turn of events that so closely mirrored that of 2009, a sluggish start and mid-season coaching change again the catalyst for a torrid end to the season and vault into contention, the Penguins once again found themselves playing for Lord Stanley's Cup when June arrived. This time there were no motivational text messages from the owner necessary as they skated out to a 3-1 series lead against the San Jose Sharks. Heading into Game 6, there was, of course, only one final piece of work to be done.

See you at center ice.

We all know how it ended. Mike Lange imploring Grandma to switch lanes, lest she be late for her bingo game. Crosby being named the Conn Smythe winner despite not scoring a goal in the Finals, a testament to his unworldly playmaking ability and unquestioned leadership that saw him become the second Penguin to raise the award while wearing the captain's C on his sweater. And of course, after the players all had their turn with it, Lemieux raising it for his fourth. Nearly as satisfying to fans as the sight of a now 50-year old Lemieux again partaking in the Penguins' championship celebration was his comment when interviewed immediately after, at center ice in San Jose's SAP Center.

Media being media in the present day and age, after fielding questions about the team and their accomplishments, Lemieux was of course tossed the inevitable question about whether winning another championship had any impact on his desire to potentially sell the team. Briefly yet succinctly he stated simply that he and Burkle were still the owners, and they were happy where they were. The following fall, days before the Penguins opened the 2016-17 season, the team's 50th, a more official statement came out.

The Penguins were no longer for sale.

The announcement was music to the ears of pretty much every Pittsburgher from Arnold Slick to Sam and his dog, a sound more beautiful than Party Hard playing every time the team scored, or the final buzzer that June Sunday night in San Jose. As the Penguins celebrated becoming one of only nine NHL franchises with four or more Stanley Cups, the impact of Lemieux remaining Owner and Chairman was clearly felt by everyone from the fans to each and every player that donned a Penguins sweater. Talk of spending to the salary cap, creating a first-class environment for players in terms of facilities, medical staff, and other assets, all rolled up into one simple mindset – an undeniable commitment to winning for Pittsburgh.

At some point Mario Lemieux will indeed skate off into the proverbial sunset. Someday he'll opt to cede his majority share of the Penguins in favor of true retirement. Despite having expressed that, regardless of what the future holds, he'd like to keep some involvement with the franchise, we all realize that just like it was impossible for him to dominate on the ice forever, it's similarly not realistic to think that he'll

Chapter 9 – "See You at Center Ice"

remain the team's chief executive for decades on end. But regardless of what that timetable may be, one thing is strikingly clear – there will never truly be a "post-Mario Lemieux era" for the Penguins or for Pittsburgh.

Since arriving over three decades ago as a fresh-faced teenager with nothing more than lofty expectations upon his shoulders and a less-than-perfect grasp of English, he's managed to leave a permanent, indelible mark on the city of Pittsburgh, arguably the least of which has been hockey-related. He dazzled and astounded on the ice and turned the Penguins from the most also-ran of professional sports also-rans into champions. He stepped up to the plate when nobody in their right mind would have faulted him for stepping away during a tremendously trying period in the franchise's history.

Above all of that however, he used his standing to positively impact the lives of so many for generations to come through the creation of his foundation and the causes it supports. In a city that has seen some of sports' all-time greats wear its colors, it could be deemed impossible to dub just one the premier of the group. But take away Mario Lemieux, and the difference in Pittsburgh – the city, not even considering the hockey team – were he to not have been a part of its history, is unimaginable.

Fortunately, it's a vision of Pittsburgh we'll never have to know.

Made in United States
Orlando, FL
08 April 2025

One More Thing…

Thank you for reading this book; I hope you enjoyed it!

If you did, there is one huge favor that I'd ask of you…

Please leave a review of this book wherever you purchased it.

Reviews help other potential readers decide if a book is something they'd be interested in and are a big part of helping authors get visibility on their work.

It doesn't take very long but goes a long way toward helping a book succeed.

Thank you again for reading!